a
Keynesian
theory
of

EMPLOYMENT GROWTH
&
INCOME DISTRIBUTION

a

Keynesian

theory

of

EMPLOYMENT GROWTH & INCOME DISTRIBUTION

Sidney
Weintraub
Professor of Economics, University of Pennsylvania

Chilton Books

Publishers *Philadelphia & New York*

To
Sir Roy Harrod
Friend
Pioneer in
Growth Economics

Preface

The ensuing pages seek to extend Keynes' ideas of aggregate-demand and aggregate-supply to the theory of growth; I had used the same concepts previously for what I think to be the appropriate version of the theory of employment. In this sense a unified theory is presented to cover both processes. In contrast, the dominant theory of output and employment tends to stress demand factors while the vast variety of growth models of recent years have tended to emphasize supply aspects, such as capital accumulation and technical change.

While employment theory holds the center of the stage, labor hire is regarded as responsive to entrepreneurial expectations of proceeds. Thus it is the enterprise sector of the economy that is examined and it is the business product which becomes the relevant income category; money dimensions are emphasized with real aspects handled indirectly. This is possible so long as the general money wage level is fairly constant; after all, this was Keynes' procedure in working out his theory in constant wage units until he was ready to analyze the effects of changing money wages. Following Keynes, money wages rising in excess of productivity are regarded as the primary cause of inflation or rising price levels and rising money income. Many Keynesian disciples have tended to neglect this part of his work; but his arguments and intuition are vindicated in the current concern with Wage Policy and Income Policy, either adopted or advocated in many Western countries to deal with inflationary phenomena.

Modern growth theory often turns on concepts of output paths, aggregate production functions, and a view of organic capital that seems so remote from the theory of the firm and microeconomics generally. The arguments below tie growth theory at each step to the firm and to the industry; after all, growth does take place within our basic production units. I am encouraged to believe that I am not mistaken in adhering to the more traditional equilibrium patterns by the appearance of Professor Hicks' *Capital and Growth*. Unfortunately, the book arrived too late to permit detailed reference.

It may be of interest to note that my work proceeded while Sir Roy Harrod was in residence at the University of Pennsylvania. Our many lengthy discussions helped me. I need scarcely add that he is a very eloquent spokesman for his own views, and that he is the best authority on how much of the argument he accepts or rejects. The dedication is meant to acknowledge his influence and friendship, and his vast contribution to the subject.

My debt to Professor Paul Davidson is very large, for his reading of an initial draft of the manuscript and for clarification of many points. I must also thank Professor Phoebus Dhrymes for taking some trouble to assist me with one argument in the text. Mrs. Gladys Decker, with Mrs. Eve McCall, puzzled over and prepared the manuscript while I was out of the country. My wife Sheila continued to display the same keen editorial interest as in the past.

Sidney Weintraub
University of Pennsylvania

August 1965

Contents

Chapter I

Growth Theory

Modern macroeconomic theory, consisting primarily of the theory of employment and aggregate output, but also involving the price level, interest rates, income distribution and, more recently, economic growth, was mainly the brainchild of John Maynard Keynes.* Especially was this true of employment and output theory; the other parts were largely fashioned out of the tools he bequeathed, often to those close to him in life, and to others as close to him in thought. Growth and distribution theory, for example, owes so much to his intellectual disciples, namely, Sir Roy Harrod and Mrs. Joan Robinson; the longer list must at a minimum contain the names of Professor Domar and Mr. Kaldor.†

Yet anomalies have occurred in the extension of the theory. Where Keynes recommended that the argument be developed in terms of employment and wage units as the key units, much of the later formulation runs in terms of real output as the main variable. Unfortunately, when this is done the effect is to discard the analysis of a money economy and to revert to the theory of a barter economy, an approach that Keynes deplored.‡ Where Keynes' theory built price level movements into its very core, the modern theories neglect them. Where Keynes held that a rise in the propensity to save could lead to *downturns* in employment, modern growth theory, at least in a careless interpretation,§ iterates the

* J. M. Keynes, *The General Theory of Employment, Interest and Money* (Harcourt, Brace and Co. 1936).
† R. F. Harrod, *Towards A Dynamic Economics* (Macmillan, 1948), Lecture 3; Mrs. Joan Robinson, *The Accumulation of Capital* (Richard Irwin Inc., 1956); E. Domar, "The Problem of Capital Accumulation," *American Economic Review* (1948); N. Kaldor, "A Model of Economic Growth," *Economic Journal* (1957) and "Economic Growth and the Problem of Inflation," *Economica* (1959). For an extension of Professor Harrod's views see his "Second Essay in Dynamic Theory" and "Themes in Dynamic Theory," *Economic Journal* (1960 and 1963).
‡ Keynes, *op. cit.*, pp. 19-20. Cf. my essay "Classical Keynesianism: A Plea for Its Abandonment," in *Classical Keynesianism, Monetary Theory and the Price Level* (Chilton Book Co. 1961).
§ These are so frequent that the models themselves must be held at fault no matter how clear the progenitors of the ideas are.

1

erroneous corollary that greater savings will mean faster growth. Finally, while Keynes was at pains to show that an underemployment equilibrium could persist, some modern growth and distribution theories simply assume *full* employment and run on in these terms.*

An Integrated Analysis

Some confusion has thus diluted the stream of modern Keynesianism, however enormous the contribution of its pioneering participants. There is a lack of unity in concept: the structure of the argument regarded as appropriate for the theory of output has been abandoned for the theory of growth. In the theory of output, demand factors such as consumption, investment, and government outlay, are stressed. In growth theory, supply factors gain the ascendency; literally each of the theories belongs to a conceptually separate world. A stride forward would be achieved if the concepts in the one were readily transferable to the other, and a common thought pattern materialized.

Ensuing pages try to do just this. Emphasis will be on employment, rather than output aspects. Employment was the important variable underscored by Keynes. In this respect there is a return to his point of view. To set the stage, we first consider the elements of the growth theory propounded by Sir Roy Harrod, for his work still dominates the discussion.†

The Harrod Equation

The Harrod equation can be presented quickly.

Starting from the Keynesian identity of savings and investment $(S = I)$, and thus the ratio of saving out of income (Y) identical with investment as a proportion of income, we then have:

$$\frac{\Delta Y}{\Delta Y} \frac{I}{Y} = \frac{S}{Y}. \tag{1.1}$$

The new term is ΔY, which denotes the *increase* of income. Writing $G = (\Delta Y/Y)$, so that G denotes the rate of income growth, and $C = (I/\Delta Y)$, meaning the *marginal* capital-output ratio or the *extra* capital

---

* Cf. the remarks of Paul Samuelson in *Keynes' General Theory: Reports of Three Decades* (St. Martin's Press. 1964), Robert Lekachman, Editor, p. 345.
† It is not too much to say that an intellectual "multiplier" has been at work in this literature. Sir Roy Harrod's original thoughts required approximately 20 pages for their presentation. Probably by now, in constant repetition and refinement, several thousand pages have appeared. This attests to the strength and merit of his seminal ideas.

required for an extra amount of output, and $s = S/Y$, then an equivalent expression for (**1.1**) is:

$$GC = s \qquad\qquad (1.2a)$$

or

$$G = s/C. \qquad\qquad (1.2b)$$

The Warranted Rate of Growth

Harrod normally attaches a subscript to interpret G_w as the *warranted* growth rate. Also, C_r denotes the *required* marginal capital-output ratio. Hence:

$$G_w = s/C_r. \qquad\qquad (1.3)$$

This equation is basic to his theory of growth.

Assuming that the savings ratio is $1/10$, so that this portion of economic resources is devoted to capital formation, and if it is the case that for \$1 of new output, \$2 of new equipment is required, then C_r takes a value of 2. It follows that G_w is equal to 5 percent. If s rises to $1/5$, then G_w would go to 10 percent. If C_r falls to 1 then G_w would mount to 10 percent in the first case and 20 percent in the second. Patently, a rise in s and fall in C_r will lift the warranted growth rate.

The formula reveals that given the savings ratio, and given the marginal capital-output ratio, then the current level of capital formation is capable of sustaining larger levels of future output. The notion of a *warranted* rate of growth enters in that Sir Roy envisages this expansion of output as compatible with the intended overall capital formation: that is, entrepreneurs install an amount of *net* investment as embodied in the s ratio and based on C_r, in the thought that demand *will* advance by this magnitude. If demand does advance in this way, then the pace of output growth is regarded as sustainable by the facts of capital formation. If output moves ahead faster than G_w, then the amount of capital put in place is below the amounts that *could* have been used, so that the economy is in the throes of a recovery and prosperity upswing in the business cycle. If the actual growth rate is less than G_w, then the capital formation has been excessive and a downward cyclical phase will set in.

Departures from the G_w rate thus have implications for economic stability and cyclical phenomena: on one side of it, there is the exhilaration of the upswing, on the other, the distress of the recession, with its attendant problems for economic policy. The system must thread its way along the delicate path of G_w for stable growth.*

* Manifestly, as all this is a very aggregative view, the G_w concept has frequently been criticized as assuming too much homogeneity in economic processes. Yet, when all is said by way of such criticisms the essential arguments still prevail: the same

One other growth rate remains, namely, the *natural* rate G_n. This is the rate of growth which Harrod contends would prevail *if the system were always at full employment*. At full employment, output would grow from year to year by virtue of the new equipment installed in the immediate past, and through the growth of population. Thus the G_n rate is the maximum rate at which the system can grow over an extended time interval even though with underemployment it is possible for $G_w > G_n$. But on this path, full employment must soon be reached. Thereafter, the greatest growth rate possible is G_n.

On the other side, if $G < G_w$ where the former signifies the actual growth of output, then recession and lower s-ratios will succeed in slowing up the warranted rate of growth.

Assumptions of Constant s and G_r

In this analysis of growth trends we have one equation and three terms: we need two other equations to complete the system. What is typically done is to assume that s is reasonably constant, and given by the forces determining the income level and income distribution. C_r is likewise assumed to be given by technological data and by the rate of interest: if there were only one production process its value would be fixed. Where there is a full continuum of processes it is a variable, dependent on going wage and interest levels. With only a few processes possible, a *spectrum* of techniques as Mrs. Robinson terms it, capital-labor shifts are somewhat more limited. Still, so long as wage and interest phenomena remain firm, and barring new technological patterns, then C_r will be fixed.

On this basis, the warranted growth path is readily determined; with three unknowns, two are settled by the economic and technological facts.

Labor Availability

The C_r concept deserves fuller attention.

To repeat, C_r is the *marginal* capital-output ratio. We can also write K_y for the *average* capital-output ratio defined as the total value of capital (K) to the total value of output (Y). Thus where $C_r = K_y$, the average ratio will stay unchanged; K_y will rise or fall whenever $C_r \gtrless K_y$. Thus we can substitute K_y for C_r, especially when C_r is constant and equal to K_y.

The use of the average capital-output ratio permits the theory to utilize a concept for which we often have good data.

---

structural neglect can be levelled at all macroeconomics. The search for total purity in concepts is likely to be destructive to all thought and inhibit any effort at immediate understanding.

Implicit in the G_w formula is the assumption that the growth in the labor force is ample to sustain the enlarged output flow. For example, suppose G_w yields a value of 3 percent. This means that new equipment installed in period t_0 supports this enhanced output flow in period t_1. But to man the new equipment there is the need for extra labor. Thus if we start with a full employment situation the labor force must grow apace, in this case by 3 percent—unless the capital-labor ratio is descending—on which more later.* The immediate point is a recognition of a built-in premise of ample labor supplies to sustain the warranted growth.

Next, to secure the G_w that is made possible by the new equipment, the output and employment determinants in t_1 must be such as to ensure that this growth will be forthcoming: the equation tells us merely of the growth *potential*. The appropriate output-employment analysis comes to us from Keynes, with some relatively minor emendations of the theory he staked out.

In sum, the theory of warranted growth must be combined with a theory of output determination and of labor growth: the theory of growth thus does not supplant that of employment. But it shows us the *future* logical consequences of the net investment that accompanies the employment level.

Interdependence of Variables

Deeper implications, involving some curious forms of interdependence, are also often overlooked in the concentration on the growth formula without due regard to the connections amongst its elements.

For example, it is often suggested that if C_r— or K_y— can be reduced, then the G_w rate can be raised, perhaps very greatly. Thus with s constant at $1/10$ say, if C_r can be lowered from 5 to 1, then G_w will mount from 2 percent to 10 percent. Fabulous growth rates are thus contingent upon measures to lower C_r. But some false conclusions may be propagated through growth arguments by this route. Let us see why.

Clearly, a lower C_r means that techniques are more capital-saving, with less equipment being used per unit of output. This being the case, we can proceed with less equipment: clearly then, opportunities for output advances by using the limited savings abound. Capital can be allotted for all sorts of projects.

But this cannot be right. For in the limit it suggests that as $C_r \to 0$, then growth prospects are unbounded! But this is nothing short of the idea that as we go back to a handicraft mode of production we can augment output indefinitely!

To drive the point home, it also means that as C_r rises without limit,

* See Chapter III.

so that more and more capital is used per unit of production and the economy becomes more automated, the prospect of output growth, rather than being enhanced, becomes stunted. The inference is that the introduction of equipment in the early days of capitalism operated to *reduce* the output advance rather than to foster it. But this *must* be wrong, for it constitutes a misreading of history with the advent of machine techniques. A formula which is capable of conveying ideas so at variance with the facts deserves a more careful rendition.

Clearly, so long as C_r is constant the relation points up the correct results. In this case, any increase in s does provide more of the same kinds of equipment and, where the labor force is ample for the advance, can sustain an enlarged output flow. In this sort of economy the only reason for limiting s would be to prevent s from leading to growth rates in excess of the population-labor force enlargement. This has seldom been a problem in the economic world so that this case can be put aside.

What then of cases where C_r falls, perhaps because of higher interest rates? Here fewer capital goods are used relative to output. It might appear that with higher rates of savings the growth process can be speeded up so that the injunction for policy might be to lift the savings ratio.

Consider what would happen in this event. Entrepreneurs would be using less equipment per unit of output. Simultaneously, more and more equipment would be brought into creation. The upshot would have to be that while a great growth is possible, savings would become so large that the demand for the final output that could be produced would turn out to be inadequate. What would be required of a falling C_r, in order to assure adequate new demand, would be a *fall* in the savings rate, so that excessive quantities of equipment are *not* constructed.

We can look at it in this way. If C_r, with a given savings ratio, should fall, then to provide for the same output expansion as before *less* equipment would be required. If entrepreneurs base their plans on a given percentage expansion, then the capital goods industries should contract, for the equipment requirements are lower. A failure to do so will mean that too much equipment is ordered and unemployment and excess capacity will be the sequel.

There is thus an interdependence between s and C_r: if the C_r requirements are lower, then the required s will also be lower.

In the alternate case where C_r goes up, capital-goods output will have to be enlarged so that s should also go up.

In short, s must adapt itself to C_r in order to accomplish the G_w rate planned by entrepreneurs. Rather than both taking on independent values, so long as G_w is the objective of entrepreneurs, and C_r is given by technological and cost considerations, it is s which must be manipulated to perform the balancing act.

A Causal Formulation

On this point of view, as s is really the dependent variable, a more apt way of writing the Harrod equation would be:

$$s = G_w C_r \qquad (1.4)$$

In (1.4) G_w is the unalterable datum: it is the output advance planned by entrepreneurs which they want realized in the subsequent time interval. Similarly, C_r is given by the input-output technology and the relative wage and interest charges on labor and capital. Thus, in order to meet the planned advance there is only one s ratio compatible with the appropriate volume of current investment.

This aspect of the analysis has been frequently confused in the argument that growth entailed simply a rising s and falling C_r— as if devoting all resources to producing capital goods in an economy that scarcely used them would be the route to output progress! Manifestly, this would be a foot-path to chaos because of a lack of demand for products.*

The Linkage to the Theory of Aggregate Income

Savings must then be adjusted to the output expansion projected by entrepreneurs: the planned output expansion is guided by their expectations of sales and profits. Capital goods orders, and the savings volume needed, must be adapted to their beliefs of future profitability.

Careless remarks about raising or lowering s therefore miss the point of the Harrod theory. For a mere expansion of s, and thus of capital goods output beyond the size required by entrepreneurs, will lead to output stagnation. It is at this stage, therefore, that the theory of growth must be linked to that of employment and output determination.

Price Levels and Depreciation Omitted

To conclude: if there is a warranted rate of growth as given by entrepreneurial expectations, and capital requirements based on these, then there is a *warranted* rate of savings, or investment, in the current time interval. Savings tendencies going beyond this will raise dangers of recession; below this, the menace of inflation of a demand variety, involving swollen profits, may threaten.†

* The same result would obtain in a socialist economy. Creating equipment for unwanted products is scarcely a mode of economical conduct.
† This is analogous to Keynes' argument in his now infrequently read *Treatise on Money* (Macmillan, 1930), Vol. 1, pp. 155-156.

Price levels are omitted in this discussion.* Of course, what is intended in the Harrod theory is a growth of *real* output so that prices are effectively eliminated from the discourse: the t_1 output must be measured in the same price terms as the t_0 output. But this is *not* strictly necessary despite the Harrod practice of doing so. For entrepreneurs do plan in terms of expected proceeds involving both prices *and* quantities, and prepare their capital budgets in money sums. We shall adopt this viewpoint in our subsequent analysis for there is no need for the theory to eliminate price level phenomena; this is an unnecessary abstraction from realism.

Likewise, while the output at t_0 is measured in net terms, this too is *not* strictly necessary, for the new equipment built in t_0 is designed for total t_1 output, and not necessarily *net* output at that date. But this is a finer point which scarcely need detain us at this stage: it will be elaborated later.

The Domar Equation

We can now examine the Domar equation and note its affinity with Harrod's formula.

Writing K for the stock of capital, Professor Domar proceeds from the following:

$$\frac{Y}{K} = \frac{\Delta Y}{I} \tag{1.9}$$

Thus it is assumed that the K_y and C_r ratios (their reciprocals really), must be equal; this becomes a condition of "equilibrium" or "balanced" growth. Multiplying by Y/Y, we have:

$$\frac{Y}{K} = \frac{\Delta Y}{I}\frac{Y}{Y} \equiv \frac{\Delta Y}{Y}\frac{Y}{I} \equiv \frac{\Delta Y}{sY} \tag{1.10}$$

and thus:

$$\Delta Y = \frac{sY}{K_y} \tag{1.11}$$

The parallel to Harrod is clear: moving the Y-term to the left, then writing G_w in its stead, by substituting C_r for K_y the identification is complete.†

---

* If the price level rises, then sales will be buoyant and activity will prove profitable; entrepreneurs will regret not having built more capacity. But this raises questions concerning the ability of the system to countenance inflation and a deflationary turn-around when price stability is established through public policy. Growth expectations can, in this event, be disappointed.

† See the early article on "The Problem of Capital Accumulation," *American Economic Review* (1948). Professor Domar's major writings on the subject are collected in his volume of *Essays on the Theory of Economic Growth* (Oxford University Press, 1957).

Thus Domar assumes that the *average* and *marginal* capital-output ratios are equivalent. Still, as the Harrod equation seems to be most meaningful when C_r is constant—and so, about equal to K_y—this is not a substantial area of disagreement. Further, in form (**1.11**) we see the *absolute* income increment that is required when new equipment is put in place with an eye to future profitability. The Domar formula also stresses the need for continuously greater annual income enlargements for an orderly pace of economic progress; each year must be the *best* year, from an income standpoint, otherwise the economy is in trouble.

Rather than subject the separate formulations to closer scrutiny, we take it that in essentials their equivalence * is established.

Employment Growth

Harrod growth theory runs in terms of *output* growth. G_w can be sustained so long as ample labor is available to operate the equipment installed. With initial unemployment, and with the growth of population and labor force, entrepreneurs can draw on the unemployment pool for the necessary labor supplies. Starting with full employment, the growth of the labor force $\left[\left(\frac{\Delta N}{N} = \dot{N}\right)\right]$ must be at least equal to G_w to permit the warranted growth rate to be sustained: thus $G_w \leqq \dot{N}$. With the inequality reversed, output growth will be limited by the labor shortage.†

Clearly, the Harrod theory is *not* one of employment growth. It will be a theory of employment growth only if real output and employment move proportionately. In general, this will not be the case; the facts of economic progress show that aggregate output has marched ahead faster than population and the labor force, so that output per capita has risen. A theory of employment growth, alongside one of capital and output growth, may thus contain some novelties of its own, and impart some extra insights.

Surely, it should do no harm to look down the road that Keynes marked out for conditions of a given stock of equipment and a given supply of labor. An employment-growth theory should extend his path.

---

* Or near-equivalence? Some disagreement is still professed. See R. F. Harrod, "Domar and Dynamic Economics," *Economic Journal* (1959).
† Taking employment initially at N_e and the labor force at N, then unemployment equals $N - N_e$. With ΔN representing the growth in the labor force, then $G_w \leqq \dfrac{N + \Delta N - N_e}{N}$. With full employment $N = N_e$.

Fig. 1.1

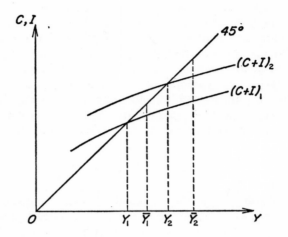

The Contrast of Output Theory and Growth Theory

As a final matter at this stage it may be well to contrast the theory of output determination and the theory of output *growth*.

For our purposes a simple Keynesian-type theory of output needs to be presented, of the type made familiar in elementary textbooks and built about the "45°-cross." * In Figure 1.1, amounts of real output (Y) are measured horizontally, and real consumption and investment magnitudes appear vertically. In period t_1, in view of the forces determining the aggregate propensity to consume and real investment (and government outlay, here neglected), the output equilibrium is at Y_1. Full employment would require a $(C + I)$ real outlay equal to $\overline{Y}_1$. Thus the forces of aggregate demand are inadequate to accomplish full employment.

As a result of investment in $t_1(= I_1)$, and the growth in labor force from period t_1 to t_2, the full employment output level for t_2 is $\overline{Y}_2$. Still, while aggregate demand is inadequate for full employment in t_2, the actual absolute output growth is $(Y_2 - Y_1)$. The maximum potential absolute output growth from t_1 to t_2 would be $\overline{Y}_2 - Y_1$ if aggregate demand grew sufficiently to absorb the t_1 unemployed plus the added labor force and the new capital stock. Full employment in both periods would permit a maximum output growth equal to $\overline{Y}_2 - \overline{Y}_1$.

The same ideas can be extended to t_3, t_4. . . . . The theory of the natural growth rate is thus concerned with the maximum rightward shift

---

* Professor Paul Samuelson, in his widely used textbook on *Economics* (McGraw-Hill, 1964, 6th ed.), has been most effective in popularizing this theory, after his initial contributions to its development.

in the full employment output. This would also be the warranted *growth* rate if full employment always prevailed and the new stock of equipment were always appropriate to the growing labor force.

There is this contrast to notice about the theory of output and the theory of output growth. The former is *demand-oriented:* output depends on aggregate demand, according to the theory. The story of growth, on the other hand, is *supply-oriented;* all its emphases are on the increments in productive capacity. This is a rather strange and complex dichotomy in theorizing. In the theory of employment, and employment growth, a unified set of concepts utilizing demand and supply ideas will appear at every turn.

Chapter II

The Theory of Employment

A capitalistic economy is one in which labor is hired by business firms in the expectation that the output of labor will be saleable later in the market place. This is the nature of the capitalistic system and it becomes the starting point for our analysis. An appreciation of this proposition is crucial to an understanding of a market economy.*

We turn now to a Keynesian theory of employment, using concepts of aggregate supply and aggregate demand. In terms which Keynes seemed to prefer, the theory runs in employment units rather than in amounts of real output: this enables us to see quickly: (1) the consequences for employment of changes in aggregate demand or supply; (2) the effect of a money wage change, and (3) the imminent distributive aspects, involving the total wage bill and total proceeds.

Until our employment-growth theory is worked out, we proceed on the hypothesis that all labor is homogeneous, all equally efficient: note that the reference is to labor that is hired in response to output and employment changes, rather than to salaried employees engaged under contract and placing a fixed charge on the firm.

A word on the labor homogeneity hypothesis: in the alternative Keynesian output models, including the Harrodian (or Domar) growth models, it is inevitably assumed that all *outputs* are *homogeneous* so that the theory proceeds in real terms. Surely there is more homogeneity at any time, and over time, amongst individuals than there is in output.†

---

* Unfortunately, this simple proposition is overlooked and economic mischief propounded in the theory of the price level, where consumers are supposed to have money to spend on goods—without the theory ever examining the source of the consumer wherewithal; the wage-earning process is simply overlooked. It is just at this stage that Quantity Theories of Money are distinguished from the Wage-Cost Theory of the price level. Cf. Chapter VIII below.
† I have criticized the output approach in my essays on *Classical Keynesianism, Monetary Theory, and the Price Level.*

Aggregate Supply

Briefly, an entrepreneur will expect from each volume of employment (N) to receive a sum of proceeds (Z) sufficient to cover his wage bill ($W = wN$), his fixed charges (F), and his profits (R), where the latter are defined in gross terms to include depreciation, tax charges, and interest payments. Executive salaries (SX) might be regarded as a form of fixed charge or a part of the profit division. Assuming they can be isolated in principle, and that they are not part of the variable wage component, a separable category can be provided for them.* Thus:

$$Z = wN + F + R + SX \qquad\qquad \textbf{(2.1a)}$$

Sometimes we shall find it convenient to use:

$$Z = kW \qquad\qquad \textbf{(2.1b)}$$

In the latter, k stipulates that the expected total of supply proceeds are some multiple of the wage bill. In the United States, for example, the total proceeds (as measured by the *Business Gross Product*) have been about twice the annual wage and salary bill since 1900.

Initially, we can treat the average money wage (w) as a constant; also, we can tie the profit level to the employment level, as $R = R(N)$: these assumptions will be examined in more detail later. Writing (w) as a parameter, the aggregate supply function (Z) is:

$$Z = Z(N;w,F,SX) \qquad\qquad \textbf{(2.2)}$$

Fig. 2.1

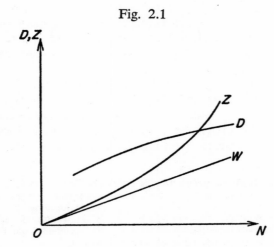

* Professor L. R. Klein properly suggested the desirability of separating executive salaries from employee compensation.

An aggregate supply function is drawn in Fig. 2.1, and is lettered Z. The wage bill (W) is drawn on the assumption that money wages are constant. If $k = 2$, and is unalterable, then Z would also be linear and rise at double the pace of W.

Each point on the Z-function thus shows the proceeds entrepreneurs *expect to recover* from each volume of employment and the concomitant assortment of goods that they in the aggregate produce. Changes in (1) money wages, in (2) the volume of equipment, in (3) the technical state of production know-how, in (4) the degree of competition or monopoly, or in (5) the variety of goods known and produced, can alter the Z-function. For the moment these factors are assumed given. Later on we shall examine the effects of varying some of these parameters; meanwhile the function is conceived in a stationary sense. The one axiom that it embodies is that entrepreneurs will ordinarily give more employment, and produce more output, *only if they expect higher levels of sales proceeds.*

Aggregate Demand

Aggregate demand (D) consists of: (1) aggregate consumer outlay (D_c), and (2) aggregate investment outlay (D_i) plus (3) aggregate outlay of government (D_g) in purchasing products from the enterprise economy. Thus:

$$D = D_c + D_i + D_g \qquad (2.3)$$

Aggregate Consumption Outlay

Consumer outlays can be decomposed according to the income categories of (2.1a) though some new income sources must be added in view of their prominence in affecting consumption expenditure. Hence, we can write:

$$D_c = c_w wN + c_f F + c_r \lambda R + c_x SX + c_g w_g N_g + (T + A) \qquad (2.4)$$

In (2.4) the c-terms denote the average propensity to consume of the respective income groups: thus c_w is the average propensity to consume of the wage earning group, c_f of the rentiers, and c_r of profit recipients, and c_x of executive personnel. The λ term refers to the "pay-out" ratio, meaning the portion of gross profits actually paid out in dividends. In the United States, perhaps about one-half of the gross profits (as defined) would consist of depreciation allowances, with one-half of the remainder siphoned off for corporate-profits tax. Of the remainder, about one-half is withheld so that ultimately only about one-eighth of R is funneled out for dividend payments. On these rough calculations, $\lambda = 1/8$, or perhaps closer to 1/7.

The symbol T denotes that some consumption outlay will come from unemployment relief, or thus out of transfer payments which are in part dependent on the employment level. Also contained in T are the sums of *interest payments on the national debt.** The A-term represents consumption outlay via dissaving, of pensioners and others relying on past asset accumulations. These sums are undoubtedly related also to the price level (P).

The more important term $(c_g w_g N_g)$ refers to *consumption outlays of government employees,* and of those receiving incomes from various *non-business* sources such as private schools and universities, religious orders, and charitable institutions. This sum is large and growing, of the order of $55 billions or more at the present time. An increase in earnings in this sector can substantially augment aggregate consumption outlay on the products of the enterprise economy.

Consumption Outlay Primarily Dependent on the Wage Bill

Equation **(2.4)** can be simplified, and the dependence of consumption outlay on the wage bill can be rendered more definite by writing:

$$D_c = cwN + c'\pi + c''T' \tag{2.4a}$$

In **(2.4a)** π denotes capitalist gross income, with F, SX, and R of **(2.4)** lumped together. Likewise, $cwN = c_w wN + c_g w_g N_g$. Also $T' = T + A$. We can surmise that T' is fairly small, perhaps of the order of 10 percent or less of the wage bill. More can be done by empirical studies to make this estimate fairly precise.†

Typical data indicate that $c = 0.9$, roughly. Hence it can be concluded that with every rise in the wage bill in industry and government $\Delta D_c = .9\Delta(wN)$.

The significance of this should be grasped for it is a phenomenon of major importance. It suggests that even with money wages constant, D_c *will rise as employment expands.* The outlay of the newly employed at the given wage accounts in great measure for the fact that the D_c directional tilt is north-east. The intercept of D_c on the horizontal axis, on the other hand, is mainly governed by the magnitude of government (and institutional) wage outlays, amounting to well over $50 billions.

The crucial point for understanding the economy is this: every rise in the average money wage (w) in industry and government will dislodge D_c parametrically, and hence D. The money wage becomes the most important element determining the position of the D_c-curve. As money

---

* While this aggregates about $10 billions currently, payments to *individual* bondholders amount to about $2 billions.

† Cf. my *Wage Theory*, p. 21.

wages increase, aggregate consumer demand outlay will expand, and almost to the same degree.*

It is in this respect that the roundabout nature of the income process is revealed, and the interaction of cost and demand phenomena is clearly discerned. For the money wage—with labor productivity—will fix the location of the industry supply curves, and hence Z, the aggregate supply function. In the same way, the D_c position is contingent on the wage level. A rise in money wages inevitably imparts an upward shove in the Z-function and a similar thrust in the D_c-component of aggregate demand. Wage payments comprise the bulk of entrepreneurial costs; the expenditure of wages constitute the main part of outlays in consumer markets. Wages are simultaneously cost and demand elements.

Labor hire in industry and government thus generates the consumption expenditure flow. Entrepreneurial decisions to produce, and to hire labor, must be the starting place for understanding the capitalistic market economy. The money wage is vital in fashioning the Z-function and simultaneously, the D_c-function. "More people at work, the wage bill will be higher and consumer outlays will be greater. Higher money wages for any employment volume will mean higher consumer outlays." This is the common sense of the theory.

Considering that $\pi = F + SX + \lambda R$, and that personal savings are relatively high for this class of incomes, then c' must be relatively small compared to c; at a guess $0.6 > c' > 0.3$.† As profits typically rise with an advance in N, then as R grows some extra consumption outlay emanates from this source: that is $(\Delta D_c/\Delta R) > O$. A rise in executive compensation can have the same general effect on $c'\pi$.

A rise in transfer payments, such as old age or veterans' pensions, unemployment relief, or personal interest payments on the national debt, will also raise the $c''T'$ aggregate. These are associated to the N-level in greater or lesser degree.

Investment and Government Outlay

We consider now the D_g and D_i components of **D**.

Government outlay (D_g) is dependent on the cost of activities undertaken by government—meaning the prices at which the necessary factors can be purchased. Rather than undertake any serious investigation of D_g we can simply assume this sum as budgeted and decided by exogenous events, and write $D_g = \bar{D}_g$.

---

* Studies indicate that wage-earners account for roughly 90% of consumer-goods outlays; the consumption function of the post-Keynesian literature is thus primarily a Wage-Earner Consumption Function. See *Wage Theory and Policy*, Chapter 1.
† Recall that π is computed *before* personal income taxes.

The D_i-function is, for our purposes, also easier to develop than D_c. Largely, we can conclude that the money investment outlay depends on: (1) the stock of capital equipment (K); (2) the profits of the immediate past (R_{-1}), and (3) expected profits (R^*). Further, D_i depends on the interest level (r) and the price of capital equipment, as well as future money wages in capital-deepening decisions. As the price of capital equipment is largely a function of unit labor costs, we can omit the price level as an independent variable. Also, where investment is budgeted largely in real terms, then D_i will be substantially dependent on price phenomena. Hence, we are left with:

$$D_i = D_i(N;R_{-1}, R^*, w, r, K). \qquad (2.5)$$

Combining the various arguments, and omitting exogenous parameters, we arrive at:

$$D = D_c(N;w) + D_i(N;w,r) + \overline{D}_g = D(N;w,r). \qquad (2.6)$$

The Aggregate Demand Function

The aggregate demand function is sketched in Fig. 2.1. Even if the D_i-sum holds constant, the D_c-component would compel D to rise to the right because of the higher consumption outlay out of the growing wage bill and greater profits as employment expands.*

Given the D and Z functions, we have two equations to determine employment (N) and aggregate proceeds (Z).

$$Z = Z(N;w), \qquad (2.7)$$

$$D = D(N;w,r). \qquad (2.8)$$

As outlay D = proceeds Z in equilibrium, we can combine equations to ascertain N:

$$D(N;w,r) = Z(N;w).$$

Solving for N we discover the employment equilibrium and then, the proceeds (Z) and outlay (D) totals.

Aggregate and Industry Supply

It is illuminating to link the concept of aggregate supply to the industry supply curves so that the tie-in to the theory of the firm is detected at every stage.

---

* For a more detailed examination of the D-function, and its shape, see "The Micro-Foundations of Aggregate Demand and Supply," *Economic Journal,* (September, 1957).

Fig. 2.2

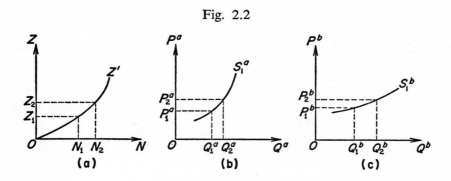

The aggregate supply function relates employment levels to expected levels of sales proceeds. A commonplace representation of the Z-function appears in Fig. 2.2a: to repeat, the argument is *that entrepreneurs will hire more labor in response to higher levels of (expected) sales proceeds.* The function assumes: (1) a constant money wage for the homogeneous labor force; (2) a given stock of equipment, so that the analysis belongs to the short period; (3) a given production function; and (4) a determinate degree of competition, interpreted initially as signifying pure competition.

It is possible to link the aggregate supply concept to the supply phenomena in individual industries, and ultimately in firms.* Thus, in Fig. 2.2a, a point on Z', such as at N_1, involves expected proceeds of Z_1. When Z_1 is expected in the economy, in industries A, B, C, D . . . etc., the expected price in any i-th industry is P_1^i and the industry supply offering is Q_1^i. Taking all commodities and all industries into account, $Z_1 = \sum_{i=a}^{n} P_i Q_i = P_1^a Q_1^a + P_1^b Q_1^b + \ldots P_1^n Q_1^n$, so that $Z = \sum PQ$. Each Z-point is thus associated with unique points on the respective industry supply curves; the Z-function thus rests on precisely the same ultimate hypotheses as do the industry supply curves.

Price and Distributive Aspects

Each aggregate supply point is associated with the proceeds *expected* by entrepreneurs; manifestly, the forthcoming demand may differ from the expected sums.† The nature of the discrepancy deserves to be elaborated.

---

* For a more extended treatment and references to the literature, see *An Approach to the Theory of Income Distribution* (Philadelphia: Chilton, 1958), Chapter 2.
† Cf. "Wages and Consumption Outlay," in *Wage Theory and Policy,* pp. 4-6.

Fig. 2.3

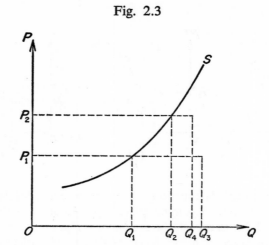

Fig. 2.3 reproduces a typical industry supply curve. At a price of P_1, the output is Q_1. Yet the amount demanded by purchasers may exceed (or fall short of) Q_1. In Fig. 2.3, at a price of P_1 *the amount actually demanded is* Q_3, so that while entrepreneurs expect aggregate sales proceeds of P_1Q_1, consumers propose to spend P_1Q_3. There is thus an *excess* of aggregate demand.

At P_2, with the expected proceeds P_2Q_2, purchasers wish to make outlays of P_2Q_4, again reflecting excess demand. At higher prices, it may be supposed that the demand quantities lie inside the supply curve of industries, so that the distinguishing characteristics are those of excess supply.

Points such as Q_3, Q_4, etc., thus trace out our concept of aggregate demand; ordering these points of *intended demand outlays* at each price, and the associated proceeds and employment level, provides the appropriate values necessary for the concept of aggregate demand. Clearly, the usual Marshallian industry demand curves are inappropriate in deriving aggregate demand for the Marshallian curves are drawn on the assumption of constant money (or real) income; the points we seek involve *varying* income levels, and thus constitute a cross-cut extracted from a family of microeconomic demand curves.*

It follows that each aggregate demand point embodies exactly the same prices as those embedded in the aggregate supply curve at each employment volume. Thus if industry supply curves rise to the right because of diminishing returns, then each successive aggregate demand point will contain the same higher prices. Each aggregate demand point

* *Op. cit.*, p. 31.

is thus linked to price and output, and thereby, to the employment volume.*

The Distributive Mechanism

The Z-function contains the income components and thus the mechanism for income distribution. For out of every Z-sum there will be disbursed wage and salary payments, and fixed payments for rents or for interest on long-term borrowing; the residual will constitute gross profits. Depreciation allowances, business taxes, dividends, and withholdings largely exhaust the gross profits category. Thus:

$$Z = wN + F + R \qquad (2.9)$$

In (2.9) the wage bill (W) is written as the product of the (average) money wage (w) and the employment level (N). Rentier income is F, and the R-remainder represents gross profits. Assuming constant money wages, the general relation of these income categories is illustrated in

Fig. 2.4

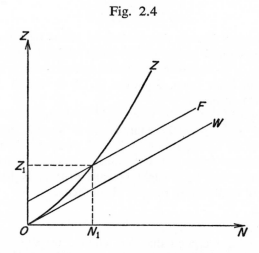

Fig. 2.4: with Z rising at an increasing pace the profit share mounts at higher N-levels. The income total envisaged in Z is approximated by the Department of Commerce data on *Business Gross Product*.

* Our aggregate demand concept thus builds on the ideas of Walras, who measured excess demand (or supply) at a given price, in contrast to Marshall who measured demand as against supply prices at given output levels in order to portray the stability of market processes. What we do in effect is: (1) to inquire of the level of aggregate proceeds *expected* by entrepreneurs; (2) to consider what this entails by way of prices and outputs in particular firms; and (3) to ask how much purchasers would like to buy at the self-same prices, when output and employment volumes are specified.

The Price Level

Largely, this is all we require at the moment to get our theory under way. But as we have built productivity, wage, and price level phenomena into our scheme it is well to have a reference equation for the price level.

The price level formulation we use makes explicit the money wage level, the degree of competition, and the productivity of labor. Thus:

$$Z = \Sigma pq = PQ \tag{2.10}$$

P and *Q* stand for the price and output levels respectively, with the small letters indicative of the microeconomic basis of the argument.*

From $Z = PQ = kwN$ we can write:

$$P = \frac{kwN}{Q}. \tag{2.11}$$

When we let $A = Q/N$, where *A* denotes the average product of labor, the basic price level formula is:

$$P = k \frac{w}{A}. \tag{2.12}$$

In **(2.12)** the *k*-term denotes the markup of prices over unit labor costs. Unit labor costs consist of the money wage divided by output per man $(= w/A)$. If $k = 2$, as the facts roughly indicate, *the price level varies directly with unit labor costs.* Equation **(2.12)** is termed the Wage-Cost Markup (*WCM*) equation.

On the supposition that the wage level holds firm, and if the average productivity of labor scarcely changes—and annual improvements in practice seem to be of the order of 2 to 3 percent—then, as we move along the *Z*-function prices will hold fairly constant, though in competitive markets there will be a slight upward drift at higher employment levels because of diminishing returns phenomena.

A Complete Model

In sum, we have argued that any change in aggregate demand or aggregate supply can affect the employment volume. Further, we shall see that when money wages are a variable, changes in the wage level are capable of influencing the course of both *D* and *Z*, and thus the employment level. Variations in the stock of capital and in the degree of competition can have the same effect. All this will have to be developed as part of a complete theory of employment growth.

---

* In the macro-approach, price and output indexes would inevitably have to be used; but we can bypass this discussion for the same problems are inherent in any price level theory.

The Elasticity of Aggregate Supply

The concept of the proceeds-elasticity (E_z) of aggregate supply will play a prominent part in subsequent analysis. Thus it will help to develop the notion at this point.

From (2.9) we have $Z = wN + F + R$. If we take it that the money wage is constant, then it follows that the slope of Z is given by:

$$\frac{dZ}{dN} = w + \frac{dR}{dN} \tag{2.13a}$$

An elasticity for Z can be defined in the usual way:

$$E_z = \frac{N}{Z}\frac{dZ}{dN} \gtreqless 1. \tag{2.13}$$

Substituting, we have:

$$E_z = \frac{w + dR/dN}{w + (F + R)/N} \gtreqless 1. \tag{2.14}$$

Hence, if the marginal profit-increase (dR/dN) in the case of an expansion of N with w constant, exceeds the average rate of fixed income and profits per unit of employment, then $E_z > 1$. This ought to be the typical outcome under pure competition and diminishing returns. Where the wage share is constant then $E_z = 1$. This seems to be the important case empirically.*

Elastic E_z values would imply that a 1 percent rise in proceeds supported a less than 1 percent advance in employment; this is what we might expect under decreasing returns. With constant returns E_z will be exactly unity. A linear Z-function, remembering that Z must start at the origin, would suggest constant marginal products although in the Cobb-Douglas case Z would also be linear despite decreasing marginal and average productivity of labor, although the ratio of marginal and average products would be constant.

The Theory of Employment Growth

This chapter has developed the theory of employment, utilizing the Z and D functions that Keynes introduced; the concepts have been neglected in the post-Keynesian fascination with output phenomena.

* In my *Approach to the Theory of Income Distribution* (pp. 29-30) E_z was defined as the relation of employment to proceeds, rather than as in (2.13). The present formulation is better suited for the theory of income distribution. The earlier formulation might be interpreted as the *elasticity of employment*.

It remains to introduce the dynamic part of the theory, namely, that dealing with employment growth. At each turn we shall have recourse to the Z and D functions outlined. Thus a common structure of ideas can be applied to both static and dynamic theories in contrast to the varying emphasis on demand in the static theory of output, and on supply in the dynamic theory of output growth.

Chapter III

The Dynamics of Investment

Growth and employment theories have now been sketched. Their contrast, in concept and units, is apparent. The obvious task is to trace out a unified system embracing both sets of ideas with especial emphasis on *employment* growth.

Capital formation is the key factor in the dynamics of per capita output growth. Of course, *aggregate* output could grow with merely an increase in population or, more precisely, the augmentation in the labor force. The latter development was envisaged by the classicists who were troubled by the Malthusian specter of geometrical population expansion while the land area remained fixed: under diminishing returns real wages were destined to hover about subsistence standards. In their model, which invited the gibe of economics being the "dismal science," any serious hope of improving living standards could not be entertained except under rare and temporary phases of "increasing returns" which could lift well-being. The more optimistic view distinguished the early American economists, notably Carey, who eyed the fertile and uncultivated lands lying westward on the American continent.*

Skipping over these ancient controversies it is indisputable that the enormous advance of our industrial society has resulted from the *accumulation* and *improvement* of capital equipment. It is no accident that modern growth theory has focussed on the volume of equipment and the state of the technological arts.

Investment and Growth

The distinguishing characteristic of the advanced compared to the under-developed regions lies in the size and variety of tools and equipment.

* See H. C. Carey, *Principles of Social Science*, Chapter IV. Cf. also the criticisms of John Stuart Mill, *Principles of Political Economy*, Ashley ed., Book I, Chapter 12.

Also apparent is an institutional learning and communicating mechanism for acquiring and transmitting knowledge on how equipment can be engaged to enlarge production. Knowledge, skills, and equipment, broadly speaking, make the difference. Natural resources often suffer from depletion, as with coal, timber, and oil; soils erode and are only partially restored through new fertilizers. So it is in new man-made items rather than in natural resources that we must look for the future gains in productivity.*

If we write K for the stock of capital, with individual components K_1, K_2, . . . etc., then the total capital stock consists of:

$$K = K_1 + K_2 + K_3 + \ldots + K_n. \qquad (3.1)$$

The essence of the theory of capital formation involves increasing the *individual K*-components. Investment (I) thus becomes:

$$I \equiv \Delta K = \Delta K_1 + \Delta K_2 + \Delta K_3 + \ldots + \Delta K_n \qquad (3.2)$$

So long as $I > 0$, the capital stock will be enlarged though some of the ΔK values may be negative, involving *dis*investment.

The Marginal Efficiency of Capital

In the enterprise economy, investment is undertaken with a view to profitability; that is, so long as items of capital equipment can promise over time to cover their capital cost plus an excess greater than market rates of interest, the project will be undertaken. The arithmetic of computing expected earnings on equipment over time, and comparing them to the capital-construction cost, is subsumed in the discussions of the marginal efficiency of capital; these discussions have been commonplace since Keynes' *General Theory* appeared.†

The Value of Capital

Representing capital by the grand symbol K hides some major difficulties in its measurement and valuation. A further comment is in order though we shall elaborate on it only briefly.

Mrs. Robinson has aptly described the stock of capital as a "who's who" of all valuable things located within an economy: everything of value goes into the census of capital, with the exception of people.‡

There remains the matter of adding the separate elements into a meaningful sum: by writing K as an absolute magnitude does suppose that the total is a homogeneous entity. Much of the obscurity and inscrutabil-

---

* Hitherto inaccessible regions may offer untapped resources for exploitation.
† A good account is provided in Paul Davidson and Eugene Smolensky, *Aggregate Supply and Demand* (Harper-Row Co., 1964), Chapter 4.
‡ Joan Robinson, *op. cit.*, p. 122.

ity of the theory of capital is in the realm of measurement. Fortunately, so far as the investment process is concerned, most of the intricacies dissolve: all of the ΔK items can be valued at their current market prices or investment cost. But when some of the ΔK items are negative, the deeper valuation dilemmas recur: should the disinvestment be estimated at original cost, at reproduction cost, market price, or some other figure? While for *gross* investment the valuation problems are at a minimum, for *net* investment, which is the difference between the positive and negative ΔK items, unsolvable measurement problems abound. Largely, as we shall concentrate on gross investment, these difficulties need not immediately deter us.

Types of Capital

Among our investment categories we have enumerated tools and equipment; the industrial plant, which houses the tools and equipment, has gone unmentioned. Yet as we examine our vast industrial complex it is the plant that immediately strikes the eye; it is also the image that is immediately conjured when we speak of a factory.

Most plants are constructed on profit principles so that the concept of the marginal efficiency of capital bears on this just as on the tools and equipment. Yet structures are often designed with more than strictly functional objectives and go beyond profit criteria. Aesthetic aspects influence the architectural complex so that a form of *capital monument,* to bespeak the taste of the management, emerges: what is being simultaneously provided is a joint capital good, and a consumer's good, for the community to enjoy. The cost of the aesthetic qualities may be nominal so that the added product comes inexpensively. Where outlays are lavish for nonfunctional adornments, the superfluities do not assist production in the same way as do tools and equipment.*

Non-Industrial Capital

Residential buildings such as apartment houses are literally "factories" producing house-space; they can be included as capital goods covered by the concept of the marginal efficiency of capital. Private homes can also be recognized as belonging to the same category, as a substitute for rental dwellings with an imputed rent being compared to the construction cost.†

---

* This is not to deny the productivity importance of well-ventilated, well-heated, and well-illuminated buildings, nor to doubt some morale aspects in working even in an architectural extravaganza. But it does suggest that when mainly architectural triumphs are sought productivity may not be directly enhanced.

† Some money value can be imputed to the range of satisfaction provided by owner-occupied real estate and the (annual) pecuniary equivalent of utility can be compared to the construction cost in order to indicate the marginal efficiency ratio. This is the usual treatment in national income accounts.

Institutional buildings, erected by government or private agencies for philanthropic uses, raise other problems, for in these instances there is generally a less precise calculation of returns measured against costs, inasmuch as the flow of services from these capital forms is not sold in the market-place: profitability figures are replaced by benefit estimates.* What is the exact sum of economic benefits from a penal institution? A rehabilitation center for the incapacitated, the mentally and physically ill? A road? A school, that contributes in manifold ways to productivity improvement and raising the quality of life? A dam? A reservoir? While more attention is devoted to such estimates nowadays, and ingenious modes of calculation have been devised, these computations are rarely likely to be accurate projections of the facts. As a result, many important items of capital are only tenuously associated with measurable income calculations.

Annual Investment in Various Capital Forms

To appreciate the various magnitudes involved, some figures of annual investment in various types of capital formation are gathered in Table 3.1.

Surprisingly, the value of industrial construction is unexpectedly small, amounting to 18 percent of the total of capital formation (line 10 in the table) or 3 percent of the gross national product. Durable equipment amounts to some 30 percent of the total or 5 percent of the gross national product. If this last total were expanded merely by $5 billions per annum we might surmise that in the modern *Affluent Society,* Keynes' prediction that the marginal efficiency of capital could be depressed to zero levels in a generation would not be far-fetched. The prediction is the more remarkable as he was writing in the days of the Great Depression of the 1930's and he could not see the huge population bulge of the post-war period.†

In part, the dilemma of *Affluent Societies* is that needs for private capital formation are relatively small and quickly sated, while the communal needs are large and growing, and are met only after exacerbated and uninformed debate within legislative chambers, often approving programs too small to achieve communal ends.‡

Consumer Durables

Consumer durables invite a word. Automobiles, television sets, refrigerators, pianos, furnishings, even books and long-lived household condiments comprise part of the list. Inasmuch as we propose to con-

---

* Rental cost of comparable alternative facilities may provide a comparison.
† Keynes, *op. cit.,* pp. 221-222.
‡ This is part of the theme of J. K. Galbraith, *The Affluent Society* (Houghton Mifflin, 1958).

TABLE 3.1
ANNUAL INVESTMENT, IN BILLIONS OF DOLLARS

	1959	1960	1961	1962
1. Gross National Product	482.7	502.6	518.2	554.9
2. Gross Private Domestic Investment	72.7	71.8	69.0	78.8
3. Total New Construction	56.3	56.6	58.6	62.1
4. New Private Construction	40.2	40.6	41.6	44.4
5. New Public Construction	16.1	16.0	17.0	17.7
6. Industrial Construction *	14.9	16.2	17.0	17.2
7. Producers Durable Equipment	25.9	27.6	25.5	28.8
8. Change in Business Inventories	6.6	3.5	1.9	5.5
9. Total 6-8	47.4	47.3	44.4	51.5
10. Total 2 and 5	88.8	87.8	86.0	96.5

* Includes industrial and office buildings, warehouses, stores, restaurants, garages, public utilities, petroleum and natural gas drilling, and farm construction.
Source: Department of Commerce, *Survey of Current Business,* July 1963.

centrate on the output of the business sector, rather than on the full flow of want-satisfying services, we omit *consumer* capital goods from subsequent discussion. The focus then is on that part of the want-satisfying process for which the money calculus most clearly is suitable. Thus all the items enumerated are counted as consumables and as final products once they are purchased. The inadequacy of the theory becomes more serious as the stock of consumer durables mounts.

Education as Investment

There are those who contend that the most important investment of all is in education, i.e., in the knowledge which improves efficiency. A literate population can follow instructions, handle communications, and in so many ways facilitate output. An educated populace can perform new technological feats which extend the state of knowledge. Statistical evidence to support this position, or even a philosophic defense of it, is superfluous: knowledge *is* a tool and it can be put to productive use, like all good tools.†

But the entrepreneurial ledger in an enterprise economy is preoccupied solely with items of capital designed either for output enhancement or the displacement of labor, and hence the augmentation of profits. Undoubtedly, industrial training is undertaken with the end of enhancing productivity and profits; but this objective can be fulfilled only if the employee remains on the job and if the wage does not mount commensurate with skill. Confining ourselves to the growth in plant and equipment undertaken with the expectation of higher future profits, the remaining pieces of theory can be slipped into place later on.

† Cf. T. W. Schultz, "Investment In Human Capital," *American Economic Review* (March 1961).

The Planned Employment-Growth Rate

Leaving these preliminaries, we now inject the dynamics of investment into our theory of proceeds and employment.

Investment for Expected Proceeds Growth

The central thought can be stated succinctly. Enterpreneurs in period t_0 make their investment plans on the hypothesis that more plant and equipment will prove profitable: while their *planning horizon* extends beyond t_1 we merely assume that the profitability accomplished in t_1 will persist.

Fig. 3.1

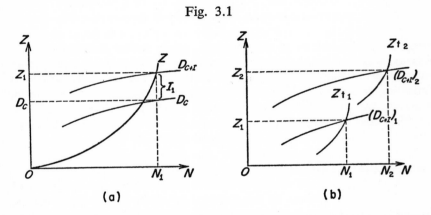

(a)   (b)

In Figure 3.1a the equilibrium proceeds for t_1 are Z_1, and employment is N_1. In the equilibrium sequence, both magnitudes are properly foreseen in t_0. Plans for t_2 invite a t_1 investment of $I_1 = (Z_1 - D_c)$. The D_c sum comprises the consumption outlay (and output) component accompanying (Z_1, N_1).

Over on Figure 3.1b, in the t_2 outcome the new proceeds point is at $Z_2 > Z_1$, with employment $N_2 > N_1$.

The warranted or expected equilibrium proceeds growth can be written as:

$$G_{ze} = (Z_2 - Z_1)/Z_1 = \Delta Z/Z_1. \tag{3.3}$$

To underscore that "today's" investment is a function of *expected* future proceeds then:*

$$I_1 = I(Z_2) \tag{3.4}$$

* In a complete time setting we would write $I_o = I(Z_1, Z_2, Z_3 \ldots Z_n)$.

Fig. 3.2

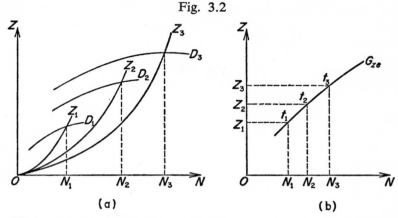

(a)   (b)

Figure 3.2a contains three sets of D and Z curves, each identified by a period designation. As in each period aggregate demand and supply expand, then proceeds and employment grow. As the investment process unfolds, the curves move rightward; for visual purposes they show a rather enormous Z and N advance—and presumably, a corresponding movement in output. For graphic clarity we have excluded overlapping curves; we shall say more on this as we unravel the several cases.*

Figure 3.2b derives from Figure 3.2a: it extracts the equilibrium points and combines them along the *equilibrium growth path,* lettered G_{ze}. As G_{ze} is extracted from the intersection of the aggregate supply and demand curves the theoretical details emanate from the same functional base used for depicting the employment level.

The link of growth to employment has thus been forged. Employment theory deals with a static state. Growth theory is concerned with the transformation of one static position into another, with investment levels generating the motion in aggregate supply.

Before exploring the schematic connections that are opened up for income, employment, capital and income distribution, we consider some other concepts useful in diagnosing a growth sequence.

Employment-Growth Elasticities

The elasticity of proceeds (E_z) referred to incremental movements along a *given* proceeds function, and related the relative changes in N

---

* The analytics of the curve movements will occupy us later. For the moment we assume that the legacy of investment, especially of the "capital-saving" variety, will place Z_2 below and to the right of Z_1. Likewise, as D_1 (and D_2) grows with the population surge, e.g., new housing, then D_2 will be above D_1.

to the relative changes in Z. We shall want to build on the same basic idea, but we must now develop it in terms of movements from old to new equilibrium supply points.

Fig. 3.3

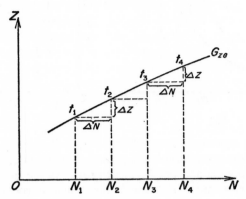

The Growth-Proceeds Elasticity

In Figure 3.3 the growth locus has been reproduced and the equilibrium points representing $D = Z$ intersections have been identified by a time date. With the equilibrium advance from t_1 to t_2 there is an increment in proceeds (ΔZ) and in employment (ΔN). It is these increments that we want to incorporate in our proceeds measure. To distinguish the measure from the earlier elasticity referring to a *given* proceeds function we term the new concept the *growth* elasticity of proceeds, and designate it accordingly. Thus:

$$E_{gz} = \frac{N_1 \Delta Z}{Z_1 \Delta N} \gtreqless 1. \tag{3.5}$$

The subscripts are intended to convey that the measurement commences at the earlier date and extends to the subsequent time interval. Clearly, this measures the movement in business income proceeds per employee.

In stationary conditions, where the stock of capital is constant, E_{gz} is likely to exceed unity, for with diminishing returns the necessary proceeds expansion will exceed the relative employment advance. In dynamic circumstances even larger E_{gz} values are not to be ruled out, for with automation and labor displacement more proceeds will be necessary to expand employment; the several cases will be considered subsequently.

The Capital-Proceeds Elasticity

Another elasticity that will play a prominent part in the subsequent study is the *Capital-Proceeds Elasticity*. This relates the *relative proceeds change to the relative capital growth*. Thus:

$$E_{kz} = (\Delta Z/Z_1) \; / \; (I_1/K_1) = \frac{K_1}{Z_1} \frac{\Delta Z}{I_1} \gtreqless 1. \qquad (3.6)$$

Manifestly, this can assume values above and below unity; it measures changes in income proceeds to the capital stock.

Combining the two elasticities we shall have a total of nine cases to untangle. On this consideration we can anticipate that the theory of growth is more complex than is customarily supposed.

All of the elasticities are amenable to measurement by rather direct statistical processes. Some tentative results are indicated below.

Capital-Employment Elasticities

The E_{gz} measure indicates the relative movements in business income per employee while the E_{kz} measure associates the relative capital-proceeds ratio. Aligning the two yields an elasticity of the relative changes in capital to the relative change of employment. Thus:

$$E_{kn} = \frac{E_{gz}}{E_{kz}} = (I_1/K_1) \; / \; (\Delta N/N_1) = (I_1/\Delta N) \; / \; (K_1/N_1) \gtreqless 1. \; (3.7)$$

From (3.7) it is clear that E_{kn} is a ratio of the incremental to the average amount of capital per employee.

Capital Ratios

Rather than working with elasticities, there may sometimes be an advantage in utilizing the ordinary capital-output and capital per head ratios.* Still, there are as many combinations among these as there are amongst the elasticities; there has been an unfortunate tendency to over-simplify this subject with an inherent confusion in basic arguments.

Definitions

By K_y we shall mean the ratio of the value of capital to business output, with the latter measured in gross terms: both sums are to be measured in constant dollars when a series of ratios is used. Concretely, K_y refers to the annual average value of the stock of business capital to the total business gross product over the same time period.

By K_n we shall mean the ratio of business capital to the average number of employees over the same period of time: K_n thus measures the

---

* We shall return to the capital-proceeds ratio below.

average amount of capital used per employee in the business sector of the economy.

Combination of Ratios

We turn now to the possible combination of capital ratios over time. As Mrs. Robinson has remarked, it is vital to keep the interrelation among these ratios ever in mind in a growing economy.* A matrix of correspondence is contained in Table 3.2.

TABLE 3.2
POSSIBLE MOVEMENTS IN CAPITAL RATIOS

K_y \ K_n	Rising r	Constant c	Falling f
Rising R	Rr	Rc	Rf
Constant C	Cr	Cc	Cf
Falling F	Fr	Fc	Ff

We consider each of the possible relations.

1. Rr: The Capital-Deepening Labor-Saving Case

In the standard case of at least early capitalist evolution, both ratios are rising. More equipment is used for each dollar of output, and equipment is substituted for labor: in short, machine-made products displace handicraft goods. This is simultaneously a "labor-saving" and "capital-using" situation.†

2. Rc: Diminishing Returns to Scale

Next, capital per head holds firm while capital per unit of output rises: this is the case of "diminishing returns to scale."

To illustrate, an increase of output by 10 percent may accompany a 15 percent increase in employment and in capital. Capital and labor

---

* Joan Robinson, "Some Problems of Definition and Measurement of Capital," *Oxford Economic Papers* (June 1959), p. 163.
† Unfortunately, these terms are used inconsistently in the literature. For some authors a rise in the capital-output ratio signifies capital-deepening while for others, a rise in the capital-labor ratio establishes this result.

are thus of diminishing productiveness as more units are applied: both labor and capital are increased proportionately, as in the hypothetical "doses" of classical theory.

This relation could also obtain through an output fall, say by 15 percent while capital and labor use dropped by 10 percent: K_y would then rise and K_n would hold firm.

3. Rf: Diminishing Returns to Labor

For a rising K_y and falling K_n several possible interpretations are open.

In a dynamic case of changing products it would involve more capital per unit of output. But it could also involve more labor. The classical analysis may be regarded as a variant of this relationship: to increase output by 10 percent may require 12 percent more equipment, so that K_y rises, and 15 percent more labor, so that K_n falls. Equipment growth thus fails to keep pace with the labor increase.

Similar results could appear in the upturn in the business cycle where output advances slowly while equipment accumulates more rapidly. If the upturn is accompanied by a reduction in the work-week, the case appears even more plausible.

4. Cr: Labor Efficiency or Capital Improvements

An output and capital rise of 10 percent, and a labor force move of 8 percent, may be attributable to an improvement in human skills, or to capital so that the new equipment is "labor-saving."

This pattern seems borne out by the facts over some periods of economic history. Over time, the capital-output ratio has often held steady while capital per head has ascended—despite the cut in the work-week which operates the other way. As many contend, the investment in human capital, in education, can account for the phenomenon. We can thus call this case one of "labor-efficiency."

5. Cc: Capital Widening

This is the standard case of the theory of growth. Here, the enlargement of output, capital, and labor is proportionate. The case is generally termed "capital-widening," whereby each fraction of output growth is accomplished by a replication of factor use. Under the circumstances, the income division also holds firm.

6. Cf: Diminishing Returns to Labor

A constant capital-output ratio with falling capital per head represents another situation of diminishing returns to labor, moderated compared to where the capital-output ratio rises.

TABLE 3.3
CAPITAL-PROCEEDS AND CAPITAL PER EMPLOYEE RELATIONS

K_s \ K_n	r	c	f
R	Capital-deepening, Labor-saving	Diminishing Returns to Scale	Strong diminishing returns to labor
C	Labor efficiency	Capital-widening or Constant Returns to Scale	Moderate diminishing returns to labor
F	Capital-saving and Labor-saving	Increasing Returns to Scale	Capital-shallowing: classical diminishing returns

7. Fr: Increasing Returns to Scale

A fall in the capital-output ratio involves, in a way, the concept of increasing returns to scale; recognizing technological progress, it may best be regarded as an illustration of capital-saving. Improvements in capital (or commodity) design permit radio sets, TV equipment, power stations, etc. to be simplified in contrast to the primitive versions of the same items. The technological advance may be so sweeping that the amount of labor and equipment per dollar of output can be cut, so that K_n rises. Compared to the capital-deepening case the investment volume over time is reduced.

8. Fc: Fixed Proportions and Increasing Returns to Scale

Whenever the K_n ratio holds firm we have an instance of fixed proportions, with a 10 percent increase in equipment involving a 10 percent increase in the amount of labor. Simultaneously, if this accomplishes, say, a 12 percent increase in output, the situation is one of increasing returns to scale.

9. Ff: Capital Shallowing and Decreasing Labor Productivity

Less equipment used per dollar of output and per employee is a "capital-shallowing" instance.

In a way, this *is* the "classical" case of diminishing returns: with the stock of equipment held constant, capital per unit of output diminishes as more labor is applied to land and equipment. Simultaneously, capital per head must also decline.

Strong movements along this line in the modern economy would be a regressive development. For example, if the cost of equipment rose to such a degree as to preclude its profitable installation, or if rising interest rate phenomena impeded capital formation, then the amount of equipment used per unit of output could diminish and the amount of labor would increase relative to the capital aggregate.

Some Trends in Capital-Output and Capital Per Head

It is well to to summarize the theoretical possibilities (Table 3.3) and determine from the data which of the situations merit most attention.

Looking at the trend of these ratios for the United States should reveal the patterns that are most rewarding for study. A brief tabulation of the capital-output and capital per employee data appears in Table 3.4. The figures refer to overlapping periods so that the trend stands forth clearly.

Table 3.4 contains some evident surprises considering that the capital-widening case is regarded as typical in the literature. Thus from

TABLE 3.4
CAPITAL-OUTPUT AND CAPITAL PER HEAD RATIOS

Period	Capital-Output (K_y)	Capital Per Head (K_n), in thousands of dollars
1900-09	2.90	$6.70
1905-14	2.83	6.76
1910-19	2.83	6.82
1915-24	2.81	7.08
1920-29	2.79	7.64
1929-38	2.88	8.03
1934-43	2.30	7.02
1939-48	1.79	6.29
1944-50	1.65	6.23
1949-55 *	1.61	6.53

* 1949, 1950, 1955

Source: *Wage Theory and Policy*, pp. 103, 106

1900 to 1929 the K_y ratio fell and K_n rose. This is the capital- *and* labor-saving case of Table 3.3.

From 1929 on, K_y continued to fall and, more astonishing, K_n also fell over much of this period. Analytically, this is the "shallowing" and diminishing returns case of our theory. Annual data for the same ratios reveal the same trends as disclosed in Table 3.4. Apparently, we must pay more attention to "shallowing" and to "diminishing-returns" phenomena than is often suspected.

Capital-Proceeds Ratios

Capital-output ratios involve $K_y = K/Z$, where the stock of capital and the value of business gross product are estimated in constant dollars.

Our elasticity formula can utilize K and Z in the same sense, with each magnitude valued in constant dollars. But this would inhibit our use of the elasticities to measure developments along a proceeds-employment path where, as a rule, prices are rising as employment expands. Let us consider the implications of changing prices.

The value of the stock of capital is $K = P_k K$ where K denotes the physical volume of equipment in constant prices. The value of Gross Business Proceeds is $Z = P_z Q$, where P_z represents the price level of gross business output and Q, the volume of output. Then:

$$K_y = \frac{K}{Q}$$

and

$$K_z = \frac{P_k K}{P_z Q}$$

Hence, whenever price levels in both sectors move proportionately, $K_y = K_z$. The difficulty arises when movements are *dis*proportionate.

As a rule, when Q rises then P_z is likely to rise. The sole effect, then, of using K_z rather than K_y is to reduce the magnitude of the capital ratio—on the assumption of P_k moving less than P_z. The worst difficulties arise whenever P_z and Q chase in opposite directions though empirically this case will be relatively rare. P_z and P_k taking off in different directions would mean capital-goods prices falling while prices in general were rising.

Whenever the capital-output ratio is intended to reflect unchanging price phenomena we shall use the K_y symbol; allowing for price movements, K_z will be employed. For incremental changes in capital stock and proceeds, the difference between the two measures can probably be neglected.

Income Distribution

We conclude this introductory survey of growth theory with some schematic relations for unearthing the income distribution aspects of any proceeds and employment level under capital growth.

The Change in the Wage Share

Neglecting the break-up of the non-wage share into rentier and profit elements, so long as we can assess the *change* in the wage share we can simultaneously understand the movements in the profit total: rentier earnings, of course, remain constant.

For the continuous case, it can be shown that:[*]

$$\frac{d}{dN}\left(wN/Z\right) = \frac{w}{Z}\left(1 + E_w - E_z\right) \qquad (3.8)$$

[*] The relation emerges by simply differentiating and substituting elasticity terms. See *Wage Theory and Policy*, p. 66.

In this, E_z denotes the proceeds-elasticity and E_w is the elasticity of money wages, with the latter defined as the relative change in money wages to the relative change in employment. Where money wages hold constant then E_w drops out and (3.8) simplifies to:

$$\frac{d}{dN}\left(wN/Z\right) = \frac{w}{Z}\left(1 - E_z\right). \tag{3.9}$$

Where E_z is unity the wage share remains unchanged, as we would expect.*

The Discontinuous Case

The preceding formulae will do for the continuous case where employment is varied in incremental amounts. In practice, however, there are generally discontinuous variations in employment and so a slight modification of the basic relation is called for. Thus

$$\frac{\Delta}{\Delta N}\left(wN/Z\right) = \frac{w_2 N_2}{Z_2} - \frac{w_1 N_1}{Z_1} = \frac{w_1 \Delta N}{Z_2}\left(1 + \frac{N_2}{N_1}E_w - E_z\right) \tag{3.12}$$

In (3.12) the subscripts refer to the successive time periods. The important modification consists of ΔN, representing the absolute change in the employment total, being written outside the parenthesis. Thus it is part of the "stability-factor"; considering the slight magnitude of $(w_1 \Delta N/Z_2)$, the ratio guarantees that changes in the wage share will be small. The old and the new employment position, N_2/N_1, becomes a minor modifier of the wage-elasticity.

An Alternate Formulation

As an alternate formulation we can always determine the wage share through use of the following equation: †

$$\frac{wN}{Z} = w_r K_y/K_n. \tag{3.13}$$

---

* The drop in the rentier share is given by:

$$\frac{d}{dN}\left(\frac{F}{Z}\right) = -\frac{F}{NZ}\left(\frac{1}{E_z}\right). \tag{3.10}$$

Relative to wages, the relation becomes:

$$\frac{d}{dN}\left(\frac{F}{wN}\right) = -\frac{F}{wN^2} \tag{3.11}$$

See my *Approach to the Theory of Income Distribution*, p. 50.

† Writing the wage-cost markup (WCM) equation for the price level:

$$P = k\,w/A \tag{3.14}$$

where w is the money wage, A represents the average product of labor, and k is the reciprocal of the wage share or mark-up of prices in general over unit labor costs, then:

$$\frac{1}{k} = \frac{w}{P}\left(1/A\right) = w_r\frac{N}{Q}\frac{K}{K} = w_r\,K_y/K_n \tag{3.15}$$

In this, w_r denotes the level of real wages, K_y refers to the capital-output ratio, and K_n to capital per head. So long as these ratios hold constant, the wage share depends on the interplay of prices and the money wage. Generally there will be some interdependence between the respective capital ratios.

Conclusion

A first step has been taken in linking the theory of proceeds-employment-*growth* to the theory of employment and proceeds; an identical set of concepts has been used for both the stationary and the dynamic phases of the theory. Investment levels have been emphasized as providing the mechanism for growth, shifting the supply functions from period to period. Augmented stocks of equipment thus move the economy along the growth path.

Appendix

Notes On The Capital Ratios

It is possible to interpret the capital-output and capital-labor ratios in terms of the constant product curves dealing with the output of a firm and representing a cross-section of the production function.* This provides another way of looking at some of the ideas.

Fig. 3.4

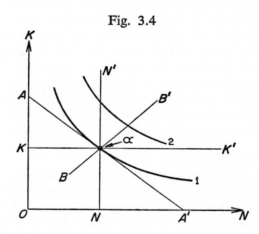

A Constant Product Curve Interpretation

In Figure 3.4, α denotes a point of tangency of isocost and iso-quant: a segment of the relevant isoquant is sketched in. Given the cost of capital and the wage rate, reflected in the isocost line AA', the output level and the factor hire level of capital and labor are determinate. Further, if we assume that the production function is linear and homogeneous, then at the given factor prices the expansion path BB' involves *proportionate* variations in factor use. That is to say, a 10 percent increase in output involves a 10 percent increment in both capital and labor.

* See my *Intermediate Price Theory* (Chilton, 1964), Chapter 3.

Along *KK'*, from α to *K'* the capital per head ratio falls; in a leftward move, it rises. Moving from α northward along *NN'* capital per head rises; going south it falls. Along *BB'* the capital ratios hold steady.

Along the isocost, moving from *A* to α, the capital-output ratio falls for capital decreases and output increases; continuing from α to *A'*, as both output *and* capital fall, the outcome is less determinate. Along the path of *AA'* capital per head diminishes.*

A Note on Capital-Deepening

Capital-deepening and a rise in capital-intensity are used here as synonymous terms. Some writers have used these terms to mean an increase in the capital-output ratio, while others have meant an increase in capital per employee. From Table 3.3 we note that in only one case do both of these relations co-exist; we termed this the "deepening" case.

One could use the term "deepening" to cover all cases of a rise in K_y. But if a fall in K_n is also involved it is doubtful if there is, in any fundamental sense, a "deepening" of capital; instead, output has become more labor-using and production has become more primitive. This hardly seems to be an appropriate instance of "deepening."

When capital per head increases the "deepening" concept might always seem to apply. But if K_y is decreasing then production is capital-saving. While this is a source of economy when efficiency in design is involved, it is a situation where "capital-intensity" is cut. In sum, the "deepening" term seems to be apt only where *both* ratios *are* rising.

Capital-Using and Capital-Saving

The major obstacle to the constant product curve interpretation of capital-ratios is that the isoquant map assumes a given state of technology. Thus it is useful for revealing the change in capital ratios with an output expansion, or with a change in factor prices. But it is almost hopeless in its intricacy for disclosing the movements under technological change where outputs may move disproportionately with given amounts of factor use as a consequence of changes in the state of industrial knowledge.

Yet statistical data do reflect technological changes as well as alterations in factor prices. Based on the quantitative historical record we are prone to speak of "capital-saving" and "capital-using" changes in technique. It is probably easier to diagnose these in terms of the cost curves of price theory than by resort to the constant product map.

---

* A similar diagram is presented by A. Asimakopulos and J. C. Weldon, "The Classification of Technical Progress in Models of Economic Growth," *Economica* (1963). They are more concerned with progress and changing functions than with a given production function.

Fig. 3.5

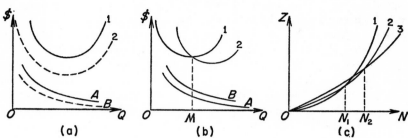

(a)   (b)   (c)

Thus in Figure 3.5a, some U-shaped *AC* curves are drawn. Curve 1 is meant to portray the initial cost experience and curve 2, the experience after a technological change that reduces production costs. With capital charges consisting of interest costs and depreciation through wear-and-tear, *A* is the curve of average fixed charges before the innovation, and curve *B,* after. One can then reasonably argue that the innovation is *capital-saving:* capital charges are lower after the innovation.

Conversely, if the *A* curve represents the new curve of average fixed costs the innovation can be described as *capital-using.*

There is one major difficulty with this analysis: the new situation is described as capital-using or -saving according to the sum of capital *charges* involved, rather than according to the value of equipment used. Changes in the rate of interest do not really concern us: both the old and new stock of capital can be regarded as financed at the same interest rate. But it is conceivable that the new equipment is more durable than the old, so that depreciation charges are less; it seems inappropriate to regard this as an instance of "capital-saving" when *more* equipment is actually engaged.

Figure 3.5b suggests that more equipment is likely to lower unit costs only at higher output levels; the new equipment can be profitably introduced so long as output levels beyond OM are normal. Again, whether the new technique is capital-using or -saving depends on the position of the new average fixed cost curve.

All this seems clear enough when the terms are used in conjunction with output levels; there is the matter of translation in terms of the aggregate supply functions. In general, if with the new techniques the new *Z*-curve lies everywhere below the old there is every warrant for characterizing the result as "capital-saving." Likewise, if the new *Z* is everywhere *above* the old we have a clear case of "capital-using," where more proceeds are requisite for each employment level to cover capital charges. Yet the usual consequence is likely to be similar to Figure 3.5b, and depicted in Figure 3.5c where for low employment levels the innovation is capital-using, and for higher employment levels, "capital-saving." This interpretation signifies that new technology can break high employment bottlenecks. The effect is to make the diagrammatic apparatus rather unwieldy when transferred to the Z-field.

Whether K_y will be higher or not will depend on the lift in K relative to the boost in Q. If output rises more than proportionately to the increase in capital stock, then K_y will fall, and vice versa. But the exact magnitudes of K_n and K_y will depend on the precise output, proceeds, and employment level in the new situation compared to the old.

All this should make us wary of capital-using or -saving concepts. Output and employment changes should generally be specified.

The Real-Capital Ratio

Sometimes the *real-capital* ratio is held to be the important concept.*

This is defined as the value of capital being divided first by the average money wage—in order to find the value of the capital in terms of standard labor—and then reduced to a per employee basis. To illustrate, if the value of capital is \$100,000 and the average money wage is \$5,000 then the capital stock is equivalent to 20 men's labor. If the equipment is used by 5 men in the production process, then each employee works with the sum of 4 men's labor as embodied in equipment: a Marxist would say that each man uses the congealed labor of 4 other men. The concept has its roots in the labor theory of value, suggesting that capital equipment is a resultant solely of labor.

A more practical reason for rejecting the concept is that it is unlikely to be more informative than the capital-proceeds ratio. To demonstrate this, the real-capital ratio is defined as:

$$(K/w)/N = K/wN, \qquad (3.16)$$

where w is the average money wage and N denotes the number of employees. Thus the concept involves the ratio of capital to the wage bill.

On the empirical fact that in the United States the wage bill holds firm at approximately one-half the value of output, we can write:

$$\frac{K}{Z} = \frac{1}{2}\left(\frac{K}{wN}\right) \qquad (3.17)$$

As the K_z ratio thus moves in harmony with the "real-capital" ratio, there is very little new information added by the latter concept.

---

* Mrs. Robinson, *Accumulation*, pp. 122-123.

Chapter IV

The Growth Pattern

Investment in an earlier period determines the growth potential of the later periods; employment and output growth are in mind here. Furthermore, the proceeds development and the price level are also matters of concern to us, as well as the enlargement of the capital stock. Growth analysis thus has at least these five dimensions symbolized by Z, N, Q, P, K. As these must always be kept in mind—with income distribution not far out of it—it is not surprising that the analysis has more than a fair share of complexities.

Needless to say, in view of the possible combination of variables, interpretation of the data is often difficult. Over time, however, they are likely to move in the same direction though at disproportionate rates. For some stretches of time the following may not be an unusual ordering of the variables:

$$\frac{1}{Z}\frac{dZ}{dt} > \frac{1}{Q}\frac{dQ}{dt} > \frac{1}{P}\frac{dP}{dt} > \frac{1}{K}\frac{dK}{dt} > \frac{1}{N}\frac{dN}{dt} > 0$$

In words, proceeds tend to move up most strongly; the employment movement seems laggard in the growth race.* Capital stock has tended to grow less than output. Price level phenomena depend on the pace of inflation.

The Growth Mechanism

It was argued previously that t_1 investment dislodged the aggregate supply function and generated the Z-N growth process. Entrepreneurial investment behavior thus becomes the key to the growth potential. But for the planned growth rate to fulfill expectations and to be "warranted" in Harrod's sense, everything hinges upon the growth in demand.

This chapter is devoted to clarifying some aspects of the growth pattern. First, the ramifications of the dislodgment of the Z-function

---

* For example, for the period 1946-1957: Z rose by about 109 percent, Q by about 46 percent, P by 42 per cent, and N by about 20 percent.

through investment is considered with respect to Q, N, Z, and P. Once the two main cases are analyzed, attention can be turned to the important growth determinants on the demand side of the equation for, after all, the full analysis is organized in terms of demand and supply concepts. The analytic foundations of Figure 3.2a and Figure 3.2b are thus examined more critically.

The Supply Variables

Let us consider the aggregate supply variables Q, N, Z, and P during the growth process. In period t_1 we take it that the capital stock grew from K_0 to K_1, with $K_1 > K_0$.

First we suppose the new aggregate supply curve to lie everywhere below the old. While the designation is not strictly accurate—for the degree of monopoly may vary—we can call $Z_2 > Z_1$ for any N the "capital-using" situation, for it implies that the earnings on capital are enlarged; $Z_2 < Z_1$ for any N is thus the "capital-saving" instance.

The Capital-Saving Complex

To validate the "capital-saving" hypothesis, *technical change must be regarded at the bottom of it all*. That is to say, through new knowledge and innovation it is possible for the representative industry to produce known outputs at lower unit costs, or to provide more output at each particular price. Output grows faster than the capital stock so that the capital-output ratio falls at each output level.* The importance of technical change cannot be exaggerated for it is *technical change which compels entrepreneurial investment*. Herein lie the dynamics of growth.

Figure 4.1 contains four quadrants with the major interdependent variables revealing different aspects of the growth process. In the *N.E.* field, Marshallian-industry type supply curves are drawn to portray price-output supply facts. Through technical progress the original supply curve S_1 is dislodged rightward to S_2.

Total-product curves are drawn in the *S.E.* field, associating output levels to amounts of labor. Despite less capital per unit of output—for output grows faster than the capital stock—the amount of capital per head at each N is higher.

The *S.W.* quadrant contains the proceeds functions. According to the figure, the proceeds necessary to generate a given employment level has fallen, for Z_2 lies inside Z_1. Similarly, the price level accompanying each Z-N level is lower while Q is larger. That is to say, at a given P, Q

---

* For a "representative industry" the index number problem of measuring output does not arise, though it may arise with respect to the stock of capital.

Fig. 4.1

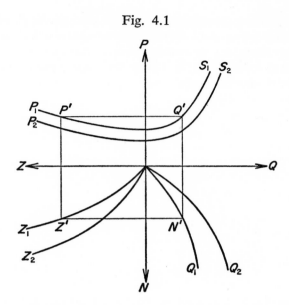

is larger, N is smaller, and Z is smaller. The price level aspects appear in the *N.W.* sector of the diagram.

To follow the chain of interdependence, we can consider the rectangle formed by $Q'N'Z'P'$ coordinates. After the supply shift, if we hold output constant, price will be pushed down, employment will be reduced, and proceeds will be lower. On the other hand, fixing P, Q, N and Z will rise. The important point is that the Q advance will outstrip the Z-N growth rates.

Symbolically, with the arrows indicating the direction, after a supply curve shift:

1. Q constant, $P\downarrow$, $N\downarrow$, $Z\downarrow$
2. P constant, $Q\uparrow$, $N\uparrow$, $Z\uparrow$

A constant price level under capital-saving will thus signalize economic expansion generally. Output constant, deflationary forces will predominate.

Output and Employment

The proposition that capital-saving sequences will involve *less* employment if output is constant seems paradoxical for it means less N with less K so that the combined amount of factor use is diminished.

This conclusion can be overturned only if the Q_2 total product curve lies *inside* Q_1. This would mean that for the new amount of K the output total would be smaller at each N. But this would be an unrealistic conclusion for over time the capital stock does increase despite indications of capital-saving per unit of output. Capital-saving refers to the latter concept, rather than to a reduction in total capital. Capital increasing, then Q would rise with each N. This is the proper conclusion to which the diagrammatic analysis leads.

Capital-Using Sequences

Capital-using sequences seem harder to rationalize. For any increase in capital which lowers costs and supply prices must reduce both the amount of labor used for a given output and the associated Z-sum. A capital-using sequence involving approximately the same amount of labor for the same output total must *raise* price and lift the Z-function in the Z-N field. But this means higher product prices despite more capital equipment; this is scarcely likely though it is conceivable with a reduced work-week. Thus in Figure 4.2, S_1 is the supply curve of the representative industry in period t_1. Suppose thereafter that money wage costs rise markedly while interest rates hold fairly constant. Further, to lend greater credibility to the situation, perhaps some penalties are attached to labor-use and some tax advantages to capital-use.

Fig. 4.2

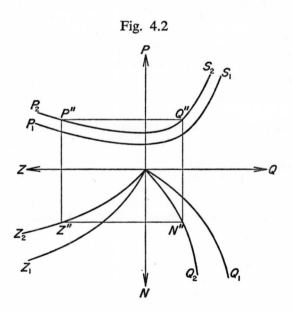

The configuration depicted in Figure 4.2 would then be possible. Combinations can occur insofar as the S-curves relate to *different periods of time,* with S_2 referring to the later situation. Note that it is a rise in money wage costs relative to interest phenomena that fosters the "capital-using" supply switch.

Of course, technical progress can also serve as an explanation for the phenomenon. Quality improvements, for example, may lead to a rise in unit production costs such as is described in the shift to S_2 from S_1: the quality improvement may be deemed to outweigh the degree of price rise for the particular quantities. Further, the quantity unit may change by virtue of the product improvement so that the Q-elements must be interpreted in an index number sense. On this basis, Figure 4.2 becomes more plausible as a description of aggregate supply events.

To summarize the interaction it reveals:

1. Q constant, $N\uparrow$, $Z\uparrow$, $P\uparrow$
2. P constant, $N\downarrow$, $Z\downarrow$, $Q\downarrow$

A constant price level would in the circumstances court economic disaster—a not surprising conclusion for conditions in which money wages rise faster than labor productivity.

The Mixed Case

Probably most important in practice, at least on the hypothesis of constant money wages, is the mixed capital "saving-using" situation; this can be related to Figure 3.5b-c in which new techniques are efficient at high, and inefficient at low, output levels. Still, so long as the equilibrium outcome is to the right of the S_1-S_2 crossing, where S_2 crosses S_1 from above, then the analysis surrounding Figure 4.1 is relevant to our argument.

The Interpretation of the Representative Industry

Before closing off this diagrammatic analysis of the growth "cobweb," a further word on the concept of the "representative industry" is appropriate.

The *N.E.* quadrant might be viewed as representative of *supply conditions in the entire economy:* the Q and the P magnitudes would then have to be understood in an index number sense.

Alternatively, the S-functions can refer to a single "representative" industry rather than to all industries. On this interpretation, which seems to correspond to our loose usage till now, Figures 4.1 and 4.2 become a miniaturization of all industry.

Ultimately, both views come to the same thing. Following Keynes we may want to argue that the Q-variable is too heterogeneous to be lumped together in one composite and that employment units alone, which are more homogeneous, need appear in our analysis. This is to insist that Z-functions alone are meaningful. Still, if we are ever to associate the macroeconomic phenomena of the full economy to microeconomic events within particular firms and industries, it is necessary to probe farther than Keynes wanted to go. Technical change, cost variations, new investment outlays, do have their impacts in firms and industries; they do alter supply functions for particular products. Hence, while we may prefer to concentrate on the aggregate Z-function, we cannot help but peek occasionally at the less aggregative supply position in industries and the cost modifications within firms. In this respect, perhaps, Keynes' view was unduly rigid.

The Course of Aggregate Demand

Now we need to inquire into the forces which are conducive to a growth in aggregate demand. For if Z shifts and aggregate demand does not follow suit, or moves in a contrary way, the growth potential may be frustrated. Only a growth in D can, in most circumstances, sustain an output and employment advance.

The aggregate demand function has been written as $D = D_c + D_i + D_g$. The separable components will have to be analyzed.

Aggregate Consumer Outlays

The consumer outlay function has been written as follows:

$$D_c = c_1 w N + c_2 F + c_3 R + c_4 SX + c_5 w_g N_g + c_6 (T+A) \quad \text{(4.1)}$$

Our purpose is to understand the shifts in this function as the clock ticks from t_0 to t_1 to t_2, etc. What must be answered is whether each component is lifted in the Z-N chart field.

A good beginning is with $(T + A)$ for the transfer, government interest payments, and dissavings components of consumer outlay can be diagnosed rather summarily.

As we move on in time, from t_0 to t_1, . . . , the total of transfer income is likely to rise. For one thing, the number of Social Security pensioners will be higher as population grows. The average pension check is also apt to be larger. Further, unemployment figures will grow (generally) in absolute amount. The number of retired people dissaving will also be greater. For these reasons, it is likely that consumer outlays $(T + A)_2 > (T + A)_1$.

Next, consider rentier incomes F. As capital goods are amassed and financed through borrowing, and as rental agreements for land and buildings rise over time, then it appears certain that in the secular sweep $F_2 > F_1$— though this need not be an undeviating annual rela-

Fig. 4.3

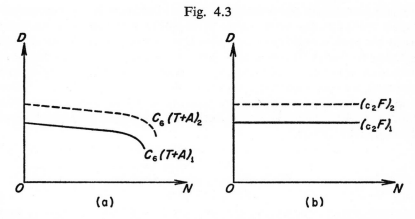

(a)   (b)

tionship. We can surmise that from this quarter the D_c-function will also tend to be elevated. This is shown in Figure 4.3b.

Profits—R—comes up next for surveillance. On the argument that $Z_2 < Z_1$ for each N-level, so that the profit share declines, consumer outlay from this source will decline.

This is based on the curve set of Z_1 and Z_2 depicted in Figure 4.1 or Figure 3.2a in the previous chapter. *But the very special nature of these assumptions must be emphasized;* it rests on the hypothesis that the money wage remains unchanged from t_0 to t_1, t_2, . . . , etc. A rise in money wages, even if the relative wage and profit share remains unchanged, *must raise profits absolutely*. Thus the aggregate outlay function from profit recipients may well be lower in t_2 than in t_1—*unless money wages rise*. For the pinching in of Z_2 under Z_1 will lower the profit magnitude associated with each N level. Only the rise in money wages over time can prevent this from happening, and sustain the outlay of profit recipients as less costly techniques of production come to be introduced.

Executive salaries (SX) are another matter. Inevitably, over time they will both drift and surge upward, and for many reasons. Not only will the average compensation mount but the number of executives will be enlarged as the scale of enterprise grows. Through time it is also nearly certain that $w_g N_g$ will go up. Even if w_g remains firm, the growth of government as population expands will enlarge N_g. In the *Affluent Society,* as government caters to more communal needs, N_g will have to grow. While w_g has an independent status its trend will be closely geared to the average wage (w) in the enterprise sector. With the march into time, therefore, D_c will edge higher in the chart field through the SX and $w_g N_g$ components.

For the wage earner portion of D_c, the argument is straightforward.

Holding w constant, the W-function in the chart field is unaffected (see Figure 2.4). On the other hand, as supply curves move to the right prices for each output level are lower; *the real income of wage earners will thus rise at constant money wages.* Conceivably, this can lower c_1 at date t_2, compared to t_1. On the assumption that wage earners save very little, we can posit that $(c_1 wN)_1 = (c_1 wN)_2 = \ldots (c_1 wN)_n$. That is to say, the wage earner outlay function will hold rather firm as Z shifts over time. Note again, the important proviso that money wages are assumed constant.

To sum up, from dissavings, transfers, and from rentiers, D_c should climb over time. Executive and government salaries reinforce the drift. But the effects from these channels can scarcely be decisive. On the other hand, from profit recipients the outlay-function should be pulled down while wage earner outlays for each N-level are unlikely to alter very much. On balance, we can conclude that if *money wages hold firm* then the D_c function over time is likely to float upward—though gently. A mildly expansory D_c trail seems to be a reasonable expectation.

Aggregate Investment and Government Outlays

The D_i and D_g segments of aggregate demand promise a more optimistic prospect of demand growth. For with technological change, and with entrepreneurs anxious to avail themselves of new methods and new products, there is reason to expect D_i to swell so that $D_i^2 > D_i^1$; the investment outlay will generally be augmented as the years roll on. With population expanding and entrepreneurs anticipating housing needs, appliance sales and demand for consumables generally, merely the "widening" aspect of economic growth would entail larger investment outlays. A steady "mushroom" lift in D_i, for these reasons, seems reasonably certain over time. Added to a price level uptrend largely conditioned by wage boosts, a projection of higher D_i-totals seems safe as a Z-N generating factor.

In a Welfare State more conscious of communal services, and the unsated needs of an *Affluent Society* more pressing, with the population bulge, with military budgets detailing the arms race and the urge for space supremacy, it seems almost inevitable that D_g, the non-wage component of governmental outlays, will climb through time. Higher price levels operate to assure this outcome.

In short, D_i and D_g provide the forward thrust in aggregate demand to sustain the new aggregate supply potential. The operation of these enhanced outlays conforms to Keynesian multiplier doctrine; the non-consumption outlays—of investment and government—have secondary effects on money income and employment. Just as these outlays are so vital for determining employment and income levels in given supply conditions, they are equally vital to usher in a growth era. Only insofar as they are enlarged will it be possible to advance the Z-N magnitudes, given the shift in aggregate supply.

Aspects of Wage Changes and Growth

The distinctive feature of a capitalistic economy is that wage earners are hired and paid a money wage. This affects the cost side of the productive mechanism, and the demand side, through D_c, D_i, and D_g. The average money wage level is thus a crucial variable for comprehending the drift in the D and Z functions in time.

Money Wages and Wage Earner Outlay

With constant money wages it was argued that the c_1wN component of D_c would be practically invariant as technical progress lowered product prices associated with each N-total. Little discernment is necessary to note that a rise in w—the average money wage—will lift D_c. Thus if $w_2 > w_1$ it follows inevitably that $(c_1wN)_2 > (c_1wN)_1$ and $D_c^2 > D_c^1$. This conclusion can only be evaded through a lower average spending propensity by wage earners, sufficient to offset the wage hike. But there is no reason to expect this; all the evidence suggests that as money wages go up, the total wage earner outlay also mounts. It would be rather strange if this were not so. The argument acquires more support when it is realized that a wage rise in the enterprise sector will also induce an increase in W_g and in SX.

This part of the argument can then be treated with dispatch: a rise in money wages over time will elevate the D_c function almost immediately and irrevocably.

Money Wages and the Profit Component

In analyzing the profit component of aggregate demand (R) it was surmised that as Z was pinched closer to the wage-bill function $(W=wN)$, profits might actually fall. This was premised on the assumption that money wages are constant.

Permitting money wages to rise imparts a new twist to the entire subject for *wage changes will determine the course of changes in profits.* It is not too much to argue that the magnitude of money profits (R) is substantially contingent on the level of money wages (w).

A proposition as far-reaching as this calls for analytic proof and empirical documentation. While the statistical verification is not undertaken here, it would be remarkable only if it did not confirm the common course taken by money profits and money wages.

Consider a distributional world in which proceeds are divided solely between wage earners and profit recipients; fixed incomes are irrelevant to our immediate analysis for they would contribute to the conclusion in suggesting the relative profit improvement at the expense of rentiers as wages, prices, and profits, rose.

We can write, where $PQ = Z$, that:

$$R = PQ - wN = N(PA - w) \tag{4.2}$$

where the average product of labor $A = Q/N$. Also,

$$PQ = kwN. \tag{4.3}$$

The latter is the price level equation (see Chapter 2) in a thinly disguised form.

Assuming Q and N constant, and k, the mark-up factor as uninfluenced by price-wage relations, then $w\uparrow$ signifies $P\uparrow$. Further, if the rise in P is proportionate to the rise in w, so that $\Delta P/P = \Delta w/w$, *this must signify a rise in R.*

The enormity of the profit rise, on the hypothesis that prices and money wages move proportionately, is worth examining. Holding Q and N constant, we have

$$dR = \frac{Q}{} \frac{\partial P}{\partial w} dw - N \, dw \tag{4.4a}$$

Assuming $(\partial P/P) = (\partial w/w)$, then:

$$w \frac{dR}{dw} = PQ - w \, N \tag{4.4b}$$

$$w \frac{dR}{dw} = R \tag{4.4c}$$

$$\frac{dR}{dw} = \frac{R}{w} \tag{4.4}$$

$$dR = \frac{R}{w} dw \tag{4.5}$$

Equations (4.4) and (4.5) should be pondered carefully: the former reveals that the profit change following the wage change will *depend on the ratio of total profits to the size of the average wage.** Equation (4.5) relates the more significant fact that the *change in profits* will depend on the former ratio multiplied by the money wage change. Thus if "profits" are \$300 billion and $w = \$5,000$, $(R/w) = \$60$ million. If the money wage rises by \$50, and prices move proportionately to money wages (with Q and N constant), then $\Delta R = \$3$ billions.

---

* The profit-term in this should include rentier incomes. Thus ΔR related to *net* profits may be quite significant.

This is a conclusion of profound importance; money wage changes are probably the prime mover in profit changes. If prices rise more than proportionately to money wages the profit outcome will be even larger, and vice versa. Prices constant ($\Delta P = 0$) the profit-fall is $N\Delta w$.

Fig. 4.4

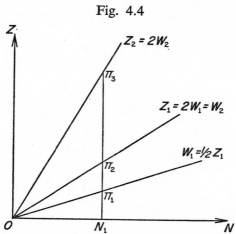

To cinch the point we can look at the argument diagrammatically. Assume a linear Z-function, perhaps accompanying a Cobb-Douglas production function.* The wage bill function is also drawn. Assume that $Z_1 = kW_1$, with $k = 2$. The curves are drawn in Figure 4.4.

Assume now a doubling of the money wage. Thus $W_2 = Z_1$, while $Z_2 = 2W_2$. While the wage *share* thus remains constant after the money wage rise, and thus the profit *share* holds firm, *the absolute amount of profits must rise*—and rather enormously. In Figure 4.4, at employment N_1 the profit increase runs from ($N_1\pi_2 - N_1\pi_1$) to ($N_1\pi_3 - N_1\pi_2$).

To conclude, as a money wage rise will generally signalize a profit rise, then the ($c_3\lambda R$) component of D_c will also be elevated by a money wage rise.

Investment and Government

By raising the prices of capital goods and items purchased by government, as well as raising civil service wages, a money wage rise will almost surely lift the D_i and D_g components of D. Insofar as *future* prices are expected to go even higher, a further lift will be rendered to D_i. Similarly, transfer payments are also likely to rise.

We can conclude unreservedly that insofar as money wages rise through time, the D-function will climb historically, so that $D_{tn} > D_{tn-1} > \ldots . D_{t1} > D_{t0}$.

* See Davidson and Smolensky, *op. cit.*, Chapter 9.

Money Wages and Aggregate Supply

A rise in money wages will drive the supply curves of industry leftward, raising supply prices for the corresponding quantities. Over time, there is the tug-of-war of technological improvements which force supply curves to the right, and money wage increases pressing the curves to the left.

Fig. 4.5

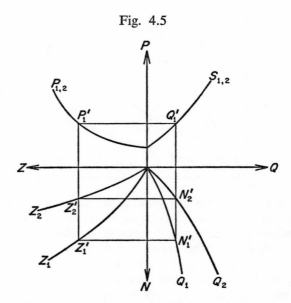

An interesting case is that in which the strength of technological advance is exactly counterbalanced by the rise in money wages so that unit labor costs (and supply prices) remain unaffected. Diagrammatically, the results are shown in Figure 4.5. While for any output level Q_1, the proceeds and price level is the same, the employment total is reduced because of the technological displacement of labor for each output volume. The Z_2 function will be pushed outward relative to Z_1 for money wages have risen, entailing higher Z-sums for each N-level.

Overlooking the neat diagrammatic feat where supply conditions are unaffected by the push-pull of wages and productivity neutralizing one another, in practice the supply likelihood will probably resemble Figure 4.6a. While both money wage and productivity increases are operative, still, the greater equipment volume will probably involve higher unit costs for small scale output volume.

Taking 4.6a as representative, the diagrammatic $Q \to N \to Z \to P \to$ sequence is given by Figure 4.1 *so long as the equilibrium position occurs*

Fig. 4.6

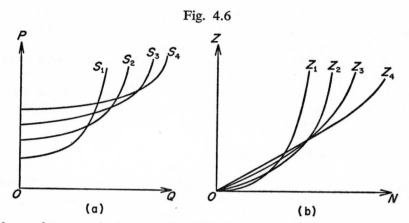

(a) (b)

along a later supply curve to the right of an earlier curve. This is merely to say that over time, the output quantities offered at each price will increase. Otherwise, Figure 4.2 is a better portrayal of the equilibrium configuration. Figure 4.6b contains the overlapping Z-curves for the criss-cross supply phenomena of Figure 4.6a.

Conclusion

The substance of the analysis is this. Technological improvements dislodge the industry supply curves rightward, while pulling the Z-function in the same way. Money wage changes operate in the opposite direction. As price levels have risen over time it can be inferred that the money wage has been master in this tug-of-war.

To sustain the growing output and employment potential created by investment, in the absence of money wage changes the great reliance would have to be placed upon growing *real* investment and *real* government outlays. The rise in money wages is likely to be conducive to even greater real outlays on investment as entrepreneurs seek to speed up capital installation in advance of future price increases for equipment through higher labor cost: the expectation of higher money wages is also likely to induce entrepreneurs to plan immediately to displace future labor and, by advance action, prepare to reduce future production costs. For the choice they face is not so much one of substituting machinery today for labor today but instead, of *substituting machinery constructed at today's labor cost for labor that will have to be hired at tomorrow's higher money wage cost.**

* Thus when Mrs. Robinson suggests that higher *current* real wages foster mechanization, the argument misses the point. For today's new equipment competes not with labor "today" but labor "tomorrow." With higher money wages, tomorrow's labor will be costlier to use relative to equipment.

Higher money wages, in the same way, drive up the D_c-function. As real wages rise because prices fail to reflect the money wage rise entirely, real consumption is also likely to increase.

Thus our analysis of a changing and growing economy is under way. The chief ingredients are: (1) increasing aggregate real investment, especially that occasioned by technical progress; (2) money wage changes; (3) increasing per capita real consumption, tending to maintain the position of D_c *even in the absence of money wage changes.*

Money Wages and Mechanization

We shall come to this point again but it is important enough to reiterate even now: largely, a rise in money wages leads to a substitution of equipment for labor when the current money wage increase is regarded as a signal of still higher *future* money wage increase. The mechanization is designed to replace tomorrow's higher priced labor with today's new equipment created by today's relatively lower priced labor compared to future labor.

Notes to CHAPTER IV

Note 1. The Derivation of the Consumption Outlay Function

The construction of the consumption outlay function is rather intricate so that some elaboration is warranted.*

Consider a "representative" industry supply function such as S_1 in

Fig. 4.7

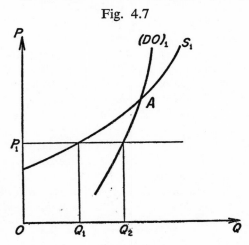

* Cf. *An Approach to the Theory of Income Distribution,* Chapter 2.

Figure 4.7. This is the appropriate starting place inasmuch as the Z-function is derived from industry supply curves. Further, our entire point of view is that the economic process is animated by entrepreneurial decisions to produce, which instantly generate wage and capitalist income.

Start with a supply price of P_1 and output of Q_1, an admittedly low output level in the industry (taken as typical of all industry) and low employment. At this low output level, with unemployment rife and transfer incomes and dissavings high, although output is Q_1 and $Z_1 = P_1 Q_1$, consumers *want to buy* an amount Q_2 and spend $P_1 Q_2$. Thus the appropiate D_c-point is $P_1 Q_2$. Excess demand equals $P_1 (Q_2 - Q_1)$.

In this way we can proceed. Lifting P_1, the new supply point and the new Z-point can be ascertained. Similarly, the D_c point can also be located from readings along DO_1. The DO_1 curve contains all the relevant demand points related to the supply quantities at each price level. Built into DO, and thus into D_c, are precisely the same prices that are implicit in the Z-function for the associated N-quantities. Essentially, *the DO function is a cross-cut of demand points isolated from a family of Marshallian-industry demand curves each drawn on the assumption of constant money income.* Along DO, as we move up from low to high prices, and low to high output levels, the aggregate expenditures implicit in DO rise.

As prices rise along S_1, and employment grows so that wage (and profit incomes) are greater, the DO_1 curve will also move in the NW-direction. But its rise will be tapered for several reasons: (1) the lesser importance of transfer incomes, dissavings, and rentier outlays as P, Q, and N mount; (2) the operation of the real-balance effect, whereby the value of money asset holdings is eroded. So long as a shift to profits occurs as the price level moves up and the S-curve becomes steeper, and so long as the average propensity to spend on consumption of profit recipients tends to decline, we can be confident that DO_1 will rise more steeply than S_1, so that an equilibrium outcome, as at point A, will be realized.

Consider then the effect of a rightward shift in S_1, as in Figure 4.1 involving "capital-saving." To derive the D_c-function, which links outlay to employment, we have to inquire as to the relation of N to Q at each P. So long as N is increased by an important advance in Q at each P, then DO will move rightward and the D_c curve will *rise* in the Z—N chart field. If N falls at each P because Q does not move sufficiently rightward, then DO will move leftward and D_c will, in all likelihood, be pulled downward in the Z—N chart field.

Note 2. Technological Change and the Price Level

More can be done to unravel the price level implications of a purely technological change while money wages remain constant.* For individual firms, under pure competition $P = w/M$ where M denotes the marginal product of labor.

There are three main cases to analyze, with some important variations in the third case.

Case 1. Marginal product of labor unchanged.

First, the marginal product of labor is unchanged at each N. On the new total product curve, the slope at each N is the same as on the old curve. For this case therefore: $P \leftrightarrow, Q\uparrow$.

As P is unchanged and output is greater, proceeds at each N level are higher, so that the Z-function moves *leftward* in the chart field, as in Figure 4.2. The wage share *must* fall; at each N the *average* product of labor is higher.† Further, as prices at each N are the same, D_c should remain rigid. Employment will thus fall unless $(D_i + D_g)$ rises sufficiently to compensate for the higher Z-function.

Case 2. Marginal product of labor lower.

Secondly, at each N, M may be *lower*. Thus: $P\uparrow, Q\uparrow$. Q *must* be higher, for otherwise there is no technical advance!

Here too the Z-function must also push leftward and the wage share will decrease as A rises for each N. Any D_c increase, what with the income shift from labor, is unlikely to be sufficient to maintain employment over time without an important supplement from $(D_i + D_g)$.

A situation of labor less productive despite technological improvements is probably an unlikely occurrence.

Case 3. Marginal product of labor higher.

Finally, it is possible that M is greater at each N. Therefore: $P\downarrow, Q\uparrow$.

In the circumstances, whether Z rises or falls at each N depends on $Z_1 = P_1 Q_1 \gtrless Z_2 = (P_1 - \Delta P)(Q_1 + \Delta Q)$, or:

$$\frac{\Delta Q}{Q_1} = \frac{\Delta P}{P_1} + \frac{\Delta P \Delta Q}{P_1 Q_1} \tag{4.6}$$

a. Thus, if the output change substantially outweighs the price change, proceeds will be greater and Z will rise to the left. The fall in the wage

---

* This section owes its origin to some comments by Professor Davidson.
† For the wage share equals M/A and in this case A rises.

share holds some ill omens for employment. With lower prices, D_c should be pulled *lower* in the chart field.

b. Where output and price changes generally work to neutralize one another, the Z-function will stay rigid. The wage share will also hold constant, while D_c may fall somewhat as prices go lower. Employment consequences are likely to be minor.

c. If output scarcely increases at each N while P drops precipitously, then Z will fall: the Z_2 function will lie below Z_1 and the wage share will rise. D_c should probably fall, tending partially to neutralize any employment advance.

This last case of a higher marginal product of labor for each N after technological change seems intuitively to be a likely outcome. Of the various alternative situations, ordinarily the output growth should outweigh the price decline. Once monopolistic elements are introduced, the (a) conclusion seems even more plausible. Hence, despite a lower P for each N, the Q increase should raise Z_2 leftward relative to Z_1.

Chapter V

A Uniform Growth Path

The variety of possible growth paths in proceeds, employment, capital formation, and income distribution can now be opened up. The theory of the Z and D dislodgments over time have been elaborated and we can now return to the equilibrium settings discussed earlier in connection with Figures 3.2 and 3.3.

As observed earlier, the possible configurations among Z, N, K and income division are more diverse than frequently supposed. This chapter concentrates upon growth paths which are steady or uniform in terms of proceeds and employment; that is, *we assume that the growth-elasticity of proceeds is unity* while the capital-proceeds elasticity ranges above or below unity. Income division and profit rates will be examined in the various situations in which proceeds per head remain constant.

A Uniform Growth Path

First, consider the growth path along which the elasticities $E_{gz} = E_{kz} = 1$. This is the standard *capital-widening* instance discussed in much of the literature. Proceeds and capital per head are thus constant.

A Linear Growth Path

Figure 5.1 traces the linear path taken by the long-run aggregate supply function (Z_g). At each date the successive equilibrium positions lie along the Z_g-line. Where the time dates relate to separate "years", although the annual aggregate supply curves need not be linear, the respective equilibrium points combine to form a linear path.*

---

* For visual purposes the growth rates have been drawn as unduly large, far in excess of the usual 2 to 3 percent annual rates found in fact.

Fig. 5.1

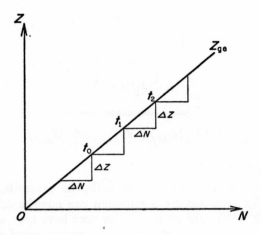

The Growth Equation: $\dot{N} = \dot{K}$

In all the linear cases, we have $E_{gz} = 1$, or $(\Delta Z/Z) = (\Delta N/N)$: the relative changes are written as $\dot{Z} = \dot{N}$. Further, with $E_{kz} = 1$, $\dot{Z} = \dot{N} = \dot{K}$. On this basis a Harrod-type growth equation can be developed as follows:

$$\dot{Z} = \dot{N} = \dot{K} \tag{5.1a}$$

Thus:

$$\dot{Z} = \frac{I_1 Z_1}{K_1 Z_1} \tag{5.1b}$$

Substituting the more familiar symbol $G_{ze} = \dot{Z}$, and writing $K_1/Z_1 = K_z$, where the latter is the capital-proceeds ratio, we have:

$$G_{ze} = \theta/K_z. \tag{5.1}$$

The symbol $\theta(= I_1/Z_1)$ refers to the ratio of gross business investment to gross business output.

This growth equation differs from the Harrod formulation only in that it utilizes the capital-proceeds ratio instead of the marginal capital coefficient; where the marginal and average coefficients are equal, the two formulations merge.* θ refers to the ratio of investment output to gross output, rather than to the ratio of savings to output; as savings and investment are identically equal the two statements come to the same thing.

---

* In this sense it is more closely identified with Domar's formulation.

Expected Growth

G_{ze}, as in the Harrod growth formula, refers to the *expected equilibrium* growth path. In period t_0 entrepreneurs are supposed to look forward to an increase in proceeds in period t_1: the expected ΔZ increase, related to the previous Z_0 outturn, constitutes the *warranted* proceeds growth G_{ze}. By assuming that the expected outcome materializes, we are dealing with equilibrium states; some remarks on disequilibrium paths will be tendered later.

According to equation (**5.1**) the magnitude of the intended growth will depend on the ratio of business investment to the value of business output, divided by the K_z ratio. The K_z ratio must be interpreted as the desired or normal relationship of equipment to sales proceeds; as we deal with equilibrium states we assume that entrepreneurs plan the correct amount of capital growth and that they predict the Z-level correctly. To illustrate, if $\theta = 1/10$ and $K_z = 5$ so that $5 of equipment is required for each dollar of gross output, then $G_{ze} = 1/50$ or 2 percent.

A Causal Statement

This way of putting matters makes the growth potential contingent upon the relative magnitude of the investment program in each preceding year's output, and the size of the capital-output ratio. The equilibrium focus also entails that the growth rate implicit in each year's capital formation will actually be forthcoming in a properly evolving dynamic equilibrium. But in the causal chain what is really crucial in entrepreneurs' minds is *some estimate of future proceeds,* as compared to present sales proceeds. Symbolically, therefore, we start with a pivotal magnitude for G_{ze}. Given the G_{ze} expectation in t_0 they undertake capital formation with an eye to larger sales receipts in t_1: the relative size of the investment program is given by θ; its effectiveness in terms of sales depends on K_z. The latter is thus an expected equilibrium magnitude. On this interpretation it is better to write:*

$$\theta = G_{ze}K_z. \qquad (5.2)$$

In (**5.2**) both K_z and G_{ze} are given exogenously: the investment term θ is then a resultant of entrepreneurial expectations concerning G_{ze}, while K_z is dependent on the technological facts which define the production function, the factor prices which govern the amounts of capital used per unit of output, and the output level expected. Once entreprenurial expectations are formed, the current investment volume will be determined.

Interpreting θ as an investment rather than a saving ratio underscores

---

* The expected employment growth can be written as G_{ne} where, on the uniform path, $G_{ne} = G_{ze}$.

the fact that capital formation is of the essence for higher growth rates. Using the savings term, as in the Harrod equation, suggests that higher intended rates of saving fosters growth. But unless higher savings compel higher amounts of investment, the result will be unemployment and economic recession, instead of output and employment expansion.*

Income Distribution

Income division in this capital-widening model can be described very quickly. As Q, N, and K grow apace, the income division remains unaffected, at least so long as money wages are constant. If the value of business output mounts by five percent, and employment grows at the same rate with money wages constant, then the wage bill matches the money income expansion. The nonwage share thus also holds its stride.

Raising the Growth Rate

Higher growth rates are possible in the linear model only through higher G_{ze} values which are implemented through higher θ ratios. Thus if entrepreneurs plan a 4 rather than a 2 percent expansion, this will require a doubling of the investment pace inasmuch as the K_z ratio is immutable. Faster growth thus requires a more optimistic entrepreneurial vision demonstrated in the form of higher investment outlays. An optimistic climate can thus lift the present Z-N position and extend the frontier of future production settlement.

A Capital-Using Path

Consider now an $E_{gz} = 1 > E_{kz}$. As the growth of capital exceeds proceeds and employment, $\dot{Z} < \dot{K} > \dot{N}$. The K_z and the K_n ratios will both be rising. The situation can be described as capital-deepening for relative to Q and to N more equipment is being used.

The Growth Equation: $\dot{K} > \dot{N}$

From $\dot{Z} = \dot{N}$ and $\dot{K} > \dot{N}$, we can write the growth equation as:

$$\frac{I_1}{K_1} = \frac{N_1}{\lambda \Delta N} \tag{5.3a}$$

where $\lambda > 1$. Hence:

$$G_{ze} = \frac{\theta}{\lambda K_z} \tag{5.3}$$

The derivation of (5.3) parallels that of (5.1) with the addendum $\lambda > 1$.

Manifestly, with $\dot{K} > \dot{Z}$ and $\dot{K} > \dot{N}$ then production is turning more

* See Chapter I.

capital-using with respect to each dollar's worth of output and to employment. In this situation one might argue that there is basically some "diminishing returns to capital", for relatively more of it is required to expand production. Probably the best explanation for the phenomenon is that production is being directed to more capital-using commodities, with the product-mix veering away from hand-crafted toward machine-tooled goods. While practically all machine-made goods can also be created by hand, undoubtedly for scores of items a labor intensive process would be precluded by cost.

The Pace of Growth

A more capital-using product-mix must slow up the pace of economic growth; the retardation will be more serious when λ is large while θ, the investment level, is firm: with a stronger swing to capital-intensive products more investment will be absorbed in outfitting each man to produce a dollar's worth of product.

While this will retard growth under full employment if savings cannot be enlarged at the expense of consumption, the phenomenon will provide greater employment opportunities under an initial situation of underemployment where the average propensity to save *at full employment* exceeds the desire to invest. As the necessary investment per dollar of proceeds growth goes higher, the prospects for full employment will be brighter. Capital-using outputs can thus raise the employment level in an economy marked by unemployment; conversely, they can slow up growth in a full employment economy.

The investment rate required to secure the warranted growth rate will be given by:

$$\theta = \lambda G_{ze} K_z. \tag{5.4}$$

As $G_{ze} = G_{ne}$, substituting the latter in (5.4) will indicate the investment necessary for a specified growth in the employment level.

Income Distribution

With money wages constant and Z-N moving in harmony, the wage and nonwage shares hold firm. Inasmuch as the volume of equipment rises faster than the absolute earnings on the equipment, the result must be *falling* rates of profit return.* This appears to be the chief distributive consequence of this model.

---

* This excludes any change in the income share of land-owners. Conceivably new equipment may replace land, rather than labor, so that the capital share can grow. But in the main the conclusion is as given.

A Capital-Saving Path

We now reverse the relationship to one in which $\dot{N} > \dot{K}$, so that $E_{kz} > E_{gz} = 1$. As $\dot{Z} > \dot{K}$, the K_z ratio falls; also K_n is diminished; this was described earlier as a "capital-shallowing" instance.

Inasmuch as $(\Delta N/N) = \lambda(I/K)$, we have:

$$G_{ze} = \frac{\lambda\theta}{K_z} \tag{5.5}$$

As before, $\lambda > 1$. As the investment rate depends upon the projected growth sequence, we have:

$$\theta = G_{ze} K_z/\lambda \tag{5.6}$$

Again, G_{ne} can be substituted for G_{ze} for a labor growth formulation.

Rather than being a rarity in the evolutionary process of capitalist development, the phenomenon of a capital "slow-down" is not uncommon for some recent times in the American economy.* We note briefly some of its implications for the speed of economic growth and then remark on the possible causes of "capital-saving."

As (5.5) indicates, given the relative investment volume θ the effect of "capital-shallowing" is to hasten the growth process; but this is to suppose that the growth process is contingent upon the investment volume, rather than the other way around, to wit, that investment waits upon the growth intentions of entrepreneurs. Enough has been said to distinguish the two propositions.

Clearly, with capital-saving in prospect, entrepreneurs have the opportunity of advancing at a faster pace in the light of the community's propensity to save; unless they avail themselves of the full employment saving potential, the inherent maximum growth levels will not be forthcoming and the chance of higher employment and greater future output levels will be partly lost. For entreprenurs will have to plan for higher rates of Z and N expansion when capital-saving techniques are available than they are compelled to do when capital-using methods are at hand; otherwise unemployment will develop. Capital-using techniques permit a slower Z-N advance to support higher present employment than under capital-saving.

A more obvious explanation of capital-shallowing involves a rise in interest and depreciation charges—which includes the practice of hasty obsolescence—relative to future money wages; the higher cost of capital would invite a search for techniques to economize in its use.

* Above, pp. 36-37.

The theme of "increasing returns," so often stressed in the theory of the firm, could also be brought into play; this would imply that for a given output and employment expansion there could be economies in the use of equipment so that capital would not have to grow commensurate with Z, Q, and N. But the most valid explanation would derive from technological progress whereby productive techniques are simplified after the initial crude innovations and experience-dictated engineering simplifications. While the first two reasons would account for capital-shallowing, it would be surprising if the last factor were not of greater importance: after major innovations come the minor improvisations designed to streamline processes in the interest of economy.

Income Distribution

Income distribution aspects follow easily enough. Constancy in the wage share follows from the unchanged money wage and the synchronized proceeds and employment movement. As the nonwage share holds stable, while capital growth slides *below* the proceeds growth, the rate of return to capital must rise.*

The Long-Run Proceeds Function

To close off this survey, we consider the long-run aggregate supply curve given the variability of E_{kz} while $E_{gz} = 1$.

Fig. 5.2

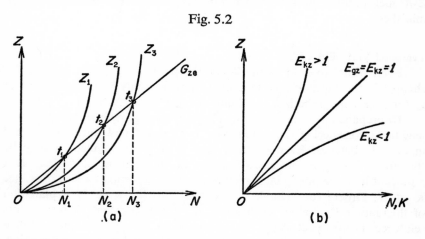

.(a)   (b)

The Aggregate Supply Function for $E_{gz} = 1$.
For the simple case of $E_{gz} = E_{kz} = 1$, the long-run supply function

* Again, rental income to land-owners is neglected.

(G_{ze}) consists of a linear path from the origin of our (Z,N) field. For $E_{gz} = 1 \gtreqless E_{kz}$, the short-period *non*-linear aggregate supply functions are intersected by the D-curves to form the linear G_{ze} path as in Figure 5.2a. Curves $Z_1, Z_2, Z_3 \ldots$ denote the time dates; as N and Z advance at a constant rate the equilibrium intersections trace the linear G_{ze} path. Despite the non-linear short period functions the wage share will hold firm over time as long as the money wage remains unchanged.

With capital-shallowing the successive Z-functions move rightward because with less capital per employee the necessary capital charges diminish though the *rate* of return goes higher. Hence from the supply side the income shift tends to favor wage earners. However, because of aggregate demand phenomena the equilibrium wage share will be unaffected.

Capital-Proceeds and Employment Paths

In Figure 5.2b proceeds are again measured along the vertical axis while *either* amounts of employment or amounts of capital appear along the horizontal axis. For $E_{gz} = 1$, the separate Z-functions are intersected by aggregate demand curves along the path indicated. Measuring capital stock on the horizontal axis, the same growth path emerges for $E_{kz} = 1$. With capital-saving and capital-using phenomena the respective Z-K curves rise at a slower or higher rate than the Z-N path: nonlinear Z-K loci become possible whenever E_{kz} successively increases or diminishes.

Temporal Variability of E_{kz}

Even while we hold to the linear E_{gz} path, it is clearly possible for changes in the capital ratios to occur. At t_1, E_{kz} may be different than at t_2, for over some periods $\dot{K} > \dot{N}$ and at other times, $\dot{N} > \dot{K}$.

Discrepancies in the capital and employment growth rates are almost inevitable considering that equipment is "lumpy" and must be ordered in discrete batches. Even when Z and N grow as planned, it may be that for a 2 percent projected increase in employment at t_0 there is a 5 percent increase in capital formation, so that in a subsequent t_2 advance $\dot{K} < \dot{N}$. Orders for "chunks" of capital provide a ready explanation of fluctuating E_{kz} values even while E_{gz} holds constant. Other factors reinforce the prospect. Viewing innovation as largely autonomous, then at some periods new ideas may be more labor- and less capital-using, and vice versa. Wage and capital cost variations also exert capital-using and capital-saving influences.

Output and Money Supply

Proceeds, employment, and capital are the key variables in our analysis. The ideas can be turned over to see what they portend with respect to physical output. Monetary implications can also be examined briefly.

Output Growth

Assuming that physical output consists of a homogeneous commodity, or that it can be unambiguously represented by an index number of output, we can write:

$$Z_{ge} = PQ = kwN \qquad (5.7)$$

Recognizing w/P as the real wage (w_r), the output equation along the growth path becomes:

$$Q = kw_r N \qquad (5.8)$$

According to (5.8) output is a multiple of the real wage bill; the excess over the wage bill constitutes the capitalist income (and nonwage payments).

So long as k and w_r hold fast, the Q path, like the Z path, will be linear: with P constant there is only a price level multiple to distinguish the two so that the one diagram could portray either function.

Monetary Aspects

Z equals the total money expenditure on current output. As the money outlay equals the money supply (M) times the output-velocity of circulation (V_z), along the growth path we have:

$$Z_{ge} = MV_z = kwN \qquad (5.9)$$

Also:

$$M = kwN/V_z \qquad (5.10)$$

According to (5.10), if V_z is constant, as supposed in the pure Quantity Theory of Money, then M would have to grow proportionately with Z_{ge}. Note that the emphasis is entirely on *the growth in proceeds as the determinant of the demand for money*. Monetary theorists would have it that Z_{ge} *depends* on the money supply. But in the enterprise economy of fact, rather than the monetary theorist's model of fiction, the system operates through labor being hired at a money wage and then, depending on the wage bargains, money is demanded from banks or other lending intermediaries. Thus a rise in the average money wage will occasion a demand for more money by business firms to make wage payments; it is not that more money *raises* the wage level, but it is instead the higher wage level and the higher price level ensuing from it which create a demand for larger money balances to finance the output volume and the associated income payments.

If V_z is a constant the demand for money moves proportionately with the proceeds aggregate. Actually, V_z is dependent on the rate of interest and the structure of income payments, their periodicity and size, as well as the motives for holding on to cash balances in different income circumstances.* Thus with a rise in velocity the money supply can expand at a slower rate during an output advance; it will have to be augmented in greater volume when V_z falls.

These ideas can be developed more minutely. But rather than viewing the causal sequence as running from money supplies to proceeds, as Quantity Theorists believe, the pattern can be visualized as flowing from expected proceeds to demands for money.†

A Golden Age

In her volume on the *Accumulation of Capital* Mrs. Robinson has pictured a *Golden Age* during which full employment prevails and capital grows at the pace given by the intentions of savers at full employment income levels.

Along the linear growth path developed in this chapter, a Golden Age, would involve $\dot{Z} = \dot{N}$, where the latter represented the natural growth of the labor force from an already established position of full employment. Capital would grow at the same rate in the simplest case so that

---

* For some analysis of income velocity, but whose image of the economic process and the price level is in contrast to these views, see Milton Friedman, "The Quantity Theory of Money—A Restatement," in *Studies in the Quantity Theory of Money* (University of Chicago, 1956), Milton Friedman, editor.

† In a passage refreshing for its candor Professor George Horwich, an able proponent of the monetary approach writes:

"Any policy calculus needs an organizing framework, and there is none better for this purpose than the equation of exchange." Also: ". . . the equation can provide a rich and ready summary of ex ante causal relationships." Further: ". . . I consider the basic premise of the quantity theory: left-side to right-side causality. In other words, a generalized or 'modern' quantity theory might be phrased as follows: the product, *MV* (total expenditures), is the cause of the product, *Py* (total income receipts or money income). The transmission is from *M* or *V* to *P* or *y* in any combination." See his *Money, Capital, and Prices* (Richard D. Irwin, Inc. 1964), pp. 447-448.

Despite the sublety, the mathematics, and the intricate argument this is all that the monetary approach amounts to; it is astonishing therefore to find thick books devoting so much space to the exposition of "modern monetary theory" when its essential ideas are ultimately so limited and so amenable to succinct statement. Cf. my *Classical Keynesianism*, etc., Chapter 3.

$\dot{K} = \dot{Z} = \dot{N}$. To ensure full employment the I-magnitude would have to be large enough to offset the savings volume that individuals intend out of the full employment income.

This raises some interesting issues on the obstacles to full employment policy for ushering in the Golden Age. When the growth intentions of entrepreneurs are strong, and savings intentions of income recipients are weak, capital-*saving* innovations can help maintain employment balance. The situation would call for higher taxes, curtailed government expenditures, and tight money if the investment surge culminated in a profit inflation.

Where the growth planned by entrepreneurs is limited, and the saving propensities are high, compensatory fiscal policies might prevent the economy from lapsing into a prolonged state of unemployment. By promoting capital-using techniques, some unemployment in the private sector can be absorbed; but the situation poses some dismal prospects for a capitalist economy.

Conclusion

Along the linear growth paths of this chapter, Z and N move at the same stride. Proceeds per employee hold constant over time. But the capital stock may go ahead or lag behind, depending on $\lambda \gtreqless 1$. With $\lambda = 1$ all variables are in harmony as in a *Golden Age*; the Harrod growth equation is particularly apt for this "capital-widening" sequence.

With $\lambda > 1$ so that $\dot{K} = \lambda \dot{N}$, a "capital-using" situation evolves. The extra capital requirements must slow up the $Z - N$ growth pace for any volume of capital formation: the higher the value of λ the smaller the proceeds and employment growth contingent upon any investment sum. Even a large investment program may have only a minor effect on proceeds and employment.

Conversely, with $\lambda < 1$ so that $\dot{K} < \dot{N}$, a relatively small increase in the investment program may yield some proceeds and employment miracles. That is, if workers require only a moderate complement of small tools to participate in the effective work force, a slight step-up in the tool output can sustain a vast enlargement in N and Z. Capital-saving techniques in appropriate circumstances can foster growth; capital-using methods can retard the $Z - N$ lift.

One final remark on λ. As $\lambda = (\dot{N}/\dot{K})$ and $\dot{Z} = \dot{N}$, then $\lambda = (\dot{Z}/\dot{K})$. Thus λ also signifies the ratio of proceeds to capital growth. When $\lambda = 1$, a "widening" of proceeds and capital is apparent. "Deepening" follows $\lambda < 1$ and "shallowing" when $\lambda > 1$.

The $Z - N$ values at any date are given by the equilibrium intersection of the $D - Z$ functions. Further, in the equilibrium sequence it must be assumed that the investment plans of entrepreneurs are fulfilled, so that the planned capital ratios evolve. Curiously, the deepening case is most likely to accomplish high employment levels because of its high investment requirements. While the immediate employment prospects are good, over time they appear more dismal in that the capital deepening presages the technological displacement of labor. After the gestation phase comes the unemployment slack. In this sense, capital-using innovations slow up the $Z - N$ growth rate, however conducive they are to immediately higher $Z - N$ levels.

Chapter VI

Nonlinear Growth Paths

Non-uniform movements in employment and proceeds occupy this chapter, starting with models in which the planned proceeds-expansion exceeds the relative employment growth. To sharpen our understanding we shall suppose that as time passes from t_1 to t_2 to t_3, . . . there is a steady enlargement of $E_{gz} \to \infty$. Alongside $E_{gz} > 1$, values of $E_{kz} \gtreqless 1$ will be introduced.

The analysis of $1 > E_{gz} \to 0$ will also be undertaken; the prospect can be identified as involving technological employment.

A High E_{gz}

Our first sequences involve $E_{gz} \to \infty$; Figure 6.1 contains an appropriate diagram.

Fig. 6.1

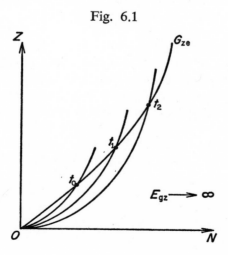

For each of the alternatives $E_{kn} \gtreqless 1$ we shall extract the relevant investment rate necessary to fulfill the entrepreneurial plans. The empirical significance of the growth path, the implicit income distribution, and the employment aspects will also be assessed.

Case 1. $\dot{N} = \dot{K}$.

First, suppose the expected proceeds growth overshadows the employment advance while capital keeps step with employment.

The growth equation emerges from the relation of proceeds and employment. Thus:

$$\dot{Z} = \alpha \dot{N}, \text{ where } \alpha > 1. \tag{6.1}$$

As $\dot{N} = \dot{K}$ we have:

$$G_{ze} = \alpha\theta/K_z \tag{6.2}$$

$$\theta = G_{ze}K_z/\alpha \tag{6.3}$$

To illustrate, if $\alpha = 2$, with the (savings =) investment ratio (θ) and the capital-proceeds ratio (K_z) given, the necessary proceeds growth is double that required where $E_{gz} = 1$. If α rises with employment a substantial enlargement of proceeds will be required to impart even a small upward nudge to employment.*

From (6.3) it is apparent that for any given proceeds-growth rate the necessary investment rate will be cut down, chopped in half if $\alpha = 2$. Clearly, this will render the task of achieving full employment in an economy with a high propensity to save extremely difficult.† By contrast to the Golden Age, it portends an almost Dismal Age for capital growth is almost unwanted despite a sales growth.

An Interpretation of the Dismal Age

As Z outpaces K, K_z must be pulled down; this can be viewed as a capital-saving sequence involving some increasing returns to capital. As K and N advance together, albeit in subdued fashion, K_n will be unaffected. Labor productivity, measured in sales proceeds, will increase.

Historically, it would not be surprising if illustrative cases were uncovered, coinciding largely with cyclical experience where the sales recovery outstripped capital formation after excess machine capacity

---

* Thus $a = f(N)$, where $\dfrac{da}{dN} > 0$. For rising rates of change, $\dfrac{d^2a}{dN^2} > 0$.

† The employment equation will be: $G_{ne} = \theta/K_z$. Obviously, employment will grow at a slower pace than proceeds.

during the depression phase. With the upturn, falling E_{gz} ratios will brighten the employment picture; E_{kz} is also likely to drop in the later stages of the recovery.

Income Division

With $E_{gz} > 1$ the wage share must fall, with the shift accentuated by large E_{gz} values; visually, the G_{ze} path will pull away from the linear wage bill. Further, as proceeds advance faster than the capital stock, the rate of return to capital will be enlarged.

Economic Policy in the Dismal Age

As capital is scarcely wanted during the proceeds advance, and as the shift in income distribution benefits nonwage earners with presumably a higher relative propensity to save, the prospects for full employment are gloomy indeed. Both factors operate to obstruct high employment: capital goods become unimportant in the productive process while intended savings run high because of the unbalanced income division. To bar serious unemployment and economic distress compensatory policies will become practically imperative. Higher values of α invite more extensive intervention in the economy.

Case 2. $\dot{N} > \dot{K}$.

Next, we consider an $E_{kz} < E_{gz} > 1$; the proceeds-capital elasticity may be $\gtreqless 1$ so long as it is less than E_{gz}. We can surmise that an $E_{kz} < 1$ presages a rather sorry economic plight.

As before, $\dot{Z} = \alpha \dot{N}$ with $\alpha > 1$. Furthermore, $\dot{N} > \dot{K}$ so that $\dot{N} = \epsilon \dot{K}$, with $\epsilon > 1$. Hence the growth equations become:

$$G_{ze} = \alpha\epsilon\theta/K_z. \tag{6.4}$$

$$\theta = G_{ze}K_z/\alpha\epsilon. \tag{6.5}$$

According to (6.4), with θ and K_z given, the $\alpha\epsilon$ terms reveal that a substantial proceeds growth is necessary to confirm the investment plans of entrepreneurs. Unless ΔZ advances by big leaps, disappointments are inevitable.

Turning the proposition around, (6.5) discloses that for any level of planned proceeds growth only a minor amount of investment is required, with the investment rate contracting when α and ϵ both grow. With the small need for additional capital goods it will be hard to maintain full employment; the difficulty will be compounded by the income distribution facts.

A Gloomy Age for Capital Goods

As proceeds grow faster than capital stock, the K_z ratio must fall; the fall will accelerate with a larger E_{kz} ratio. When the latter becomes truly large even a substantial increase in Business Gross Product will fail to stimulate new capital formation. Further, as $\dot{N} > \dot{K}$, the K_n figure will fall.

Essentially, this case is one of "capital-shallowing." Excess capacity, technological improvements, or a rise in capital costs can account for the capital-saving; as variants of the case were encountered earlier, further elaboration is unnecessary.

This situation portends a gloomy outlook for the capital goods industries, especially as ϵ becomes larger; as E_{kz} mounts the employment consequences can become disastrous, for labor use may scarcely advance despite the proceeds-growth; the investment activity may be at a stand-still even as savings tendencies run strong. Strong measures of public policy may have to be invoked to prevent the system from running down on the employment front. The employment-growth equation $G_{ne} = \epsilon\theta/\alpha K_z$ indicates the slow-down of employment as against proceeds.

Income Distribution

The income shift will be decidedly toward non-wage recipients. However, as the pace of capital formation slows, the rate of return on capital goods will go up. This is the anomaly: scarcely any capital goods are required and yet the earning power of capital may be high. Rather than concluding that this is an absurd contradiction, it may be ascribed to a tendency of capitalists to insist upon higher income prospects before they order new capital equipment at a time when the technical need for equipment is low. The dire state of affairs can be self-reinforcing: economic conditions are likely to compel public intervention in order to maintain higher employment levels. But the same actions may make entrepreneurs timid and induce them to wait for higher rates of return. Public efforts to facilitate the absorption of labor by private enterprise can thereby be frustrated.

One qualification may be appended to this unseemly combination of very high rates of return and a very low inducement to invest. The capital-returns deduced in our analysis is a *gross* figure computed *before* corporate and personal income taxes. This makes the case somewhat more plausible for it is *net* returns after taxes which foster or retard investment. But to understand the distributive forces in the enterprise economy it is best that we work with *gross* categories; otherwise we would also have to treat wage earnings only *after* taxes.

Case 3. $\dot{K} > \dot{N}$.

With $E_{gz} > 1 < E_{kn}$ or $\dot{K} > \dot{N}$, the outlook is distinctly more favorable to high level employment, especially if $E_{kz} \approx E_{gz}$.

But the relations may also be distinctly unfavorable to an employment *advance* for both elasticities suggest a low employment upswing. Everything hinges upon: (1) the growth of the labor force and (2) the initial unemployment, as well as (3) the elasticity magnitudes. Starting from nearly full employment, where the labor force grows slowly, full employment and even boom tendencies may appear. This might be christened a Glorious Age. Commencing with severe unemployment, the economy may exhibit some strains of despair from an employment standpoint unless this incipient Desperate Age alleviates its problems by contracting the work-week and transforming itself into a Leisure Age to erase its unemployment ills. The slow employment growth is attributable to the technological displacement of labor.

The relevant growth equations are:

$$G_{ze} = \alpha\theta/\epsilon K_z. \tag{6.6}$$

$$\theta = \epsilon G_{ze}K_z/\alpha \tag{6.7}$$

Everything is thus contingent upon the size of α and ϵ. If they are equal, then we are back in the "widening" case where capital and employment grow apace, and proportionately with proceeds.* By assumption, as proceeds grow faster than employment then $\alpha \gtreqless \epsilon$.

Where α is the larger, so that the capital growth outstrips employment, the result is distinctly favorable to high *levels* of employment and the economy may verge on inflation; the relation may also prevail in conditions in which the increase in the labor force is small, perhaps accomplished by a cut in the work-week. Conceivably, $E_{kz} > E_{gz}$; this can happen when new equipment is highly labor-saving. Automation can be read into these remarks; labor-saving innovation is thus a desirable concomitant of an economy in which the labor force is slow to grow. It is a more insidious employment factor in an economy in which the labor force is growing rapidly, especially if the innovations are capital-saving while labor-displacing, perhaps stimulated by labor markets in which money wages are expected to rise excessively over time compared to capital charges.

---

* As $G_{ne} = \theta/\epsilon K_z$ the situation is favorable to employment only if $\epsilon < 1$.

Labor Savings Aspects

As $\dot{K} > \dot{N}$, the $\dot{K}_n$ ratio will rise. On the other hand, as $\dot{K} \gtreqless \dot{Z}$ the new K_z ratio is indeterminate: a deepening case emerges where capital grows faster, a "labor-efficiency" illustration where K_z holds constant, and an "increasing-returns" instance where K_z grows slower than proceeds. In each instance there is a rise in capital stock per employee.

Income Distribution

That the wage share will fall is certain. The capital share will rise but conclusions about the rate of (gross) return depend on the magnitude of the upward thrust of capital relative to nonwage income. All return rates are possible, on *a priori* grounds.

Empirical Evidence of the Increase in the Capital Share

The likelihood of an $E_{gz} > 1$ may be inferred from the facts on income distribution; the high elasticity compels a shift in the income distribution from labor to capital. Using the available data on the wage share, Table 6.1 permits some inferences on the nonwage share. While the trend since 1929 has been moderately downward, the share of capital increased in some years so that $E_{gz} > 1$ is more than a theoretical possibility though not as prominent as a hypothesis of a constant or a rising wage share.

Fig 6.2

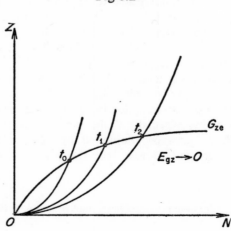

A Low E_{gz}

An employment-proceeds elasticity below unity entails a rising wage share over time. Assuming that E_{gz} falls continuously, though gradually, Figure 6.2 contains an appropriate diagrammatic picture. The analysis can be condensed in view of our familiarity with E_{gz} growth models.

Case 1. $\dot{N} = \dot{K}$.

This seems to be a peculiar case to diagnose, for if we think about it, it involves a 2 percent increase in employment and capital equipment for a 1 percent increase in sales proceeds—or $E_{gz} = 1/2$, for illustrative purposes.

It is hard to make economic sense of this. For if the individual supply curves in the separate firms are rising steeply, small increases in

TABLE 6.1

THE NONWAGE SHARE IN BUSINESS GROSS PRODUCT,
1929-1960

	Ratio	*Annual Change*		*Ratio*	*Annual Change*
1929	53.8	—	1944	51.1	+0.7
1930	51.8	−2.0	1945	51.6	+0.5
1931	52.3	+0.5	1946	49.8	−1.8
1932	51.7	−0.6	1947	49.2	−0.6
1933	52.4	+0.7	1948	49.6	+0.4
1934	52.6	+0.2	1949	49.8	+0.2
1935	53.7	+1.1	1950	50.0	+0.2
1936	53.6	−0.1	1951	49.8	−0.2
1937	51.9	−1.7	1952	48.5	−1.3
1938	52.6	+0.7	1953	47.3	−1.2
1939	52.3	−0.3	1954	47.3	0.0
1940	53.0	−0.3	1955	48.1	+0.8
1941	53.1	+0.1	1956	46.5	−1.6
1942	52.0	−1.1	1957	46.4	−0.1
1943	50.4	−1.6	1958	46.8	+0.4
			1959	46.8	0.0
			1960	46.4	−0.4

Source: Department of Commerce, *U.S. Income and Output* (1959), pp. 134-135, 138-139; *Survey of Current Business* (July 1961).

output and large increases in employment are possible, as under diminishing returns. But this would also entail sharply rising supply prices for output and, thus, a large proceeds-elasticity in excess of unity.

Fig 6.3

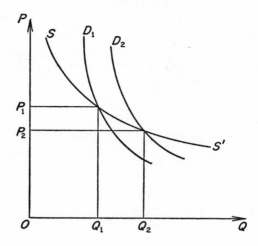

Increasing returns would involve supply curves falling to the right. This hypothesis is illustrated in Figure 6.3, with SS' denoting the supply curve, and two successive demand curves drawn with their corresponding proceeds rectangles showing a minor enlargement in purchase outlays.

This would be an intelligible phenomenon were it not for one fact, namely, that a decreasing supply curve presupposes that while labor increases less than proportionately with output, capital equipment holds constant. Yet on our assumptions capital is also increasing—and at a pace equal to that of labor!

While we may remain skeptical of this case and regard it simply as an intellectual exercise at the present time, the pertinent growth equation is:

$$G_{ze} = \theta/\alpha K_z \tag{6.8}$$

$$\theta = \alpha G_{ze} K_z \tag{6.9}$$

Thus, given the investment rate the α-term serves to slow up the proceeds growth rate. Alternatively, a given proceeds expectation necessitates an investment volume elevated by virtue of the α-parameter.

As capital outstrips proceeds growth, the K_z ratio will fall. Capital and employment moving apace, K_n will be constant.* This outcome could only denote increasing returns to scale, where the extra output was attributable not to changed ratios of factor use—for this is ruled out by the constant amount of capital per head—but to a reorganization

---

* That $\dot{N} > \dot{Z}$ may be discerned from $G_{ne} = \theta/K_z$.

of the work process resulting in some economies of scale. Strained reasoning of this sort might impart some economic sense to this case.

Income Distribution

That $E_{gz} < 1$ is enough to reveal the income shift to labor from nonwage categories. As capital grows proportionately with labor, while nonwage proceeds fail to keep the pace, the gross rate of return to capital must fall.

Policy Aspects

The specified elasticities promise an employment Glory Age: a very small proceeds expectation accomplishes a rather sharp increase in employment and in capital formation. Full employment prospects are simply rosy—if only entrepreneurs can be persuaded to order large blocks of equipment, despite scarcely any increase in sales proceeds, while faced with dwindling rates of (gross) return on new investment.

Case 2. $\dot{K} > \dot{N}$.

This is an even more dubious image than the previous one; it involves employment advancing faster than proceeds, but capital climbing faster than both! A 1 percent expected proceeds advance leads, say, to a 2 percent employment advance, and a 3 percent jump in capital equipment.

It is pointless to pursue the analysis to any length. The growth equations are:

$$G_{ze} = \theta/\alpha\epsilon K_z \qquad (6.10)$$

$$\theta = \alpha\epsilon G_{ze}K_z \qquad (6.11)$$

With growth, K_z and K_n will go up. Income will be diverted to labor and the rate of capital return will decline.

Case 3. $\dot{N} > \dot{K}$.

Employment growing faster than either proceeds or capital deserves only a brief analysis. The growth formulae are:

$$G_{ze} = \epsilon\theta/\alpha K_z \qquad (6.12)$$

$$\theta = \alpha G_{ze}K_z/\epsilon \qquad (6.13)$$

Again, the outcome depends on α and ϵ. If they are nearly equal, meaning that $E_{gz} \approx 1/E_{kz}$, so that employment and proceeds growth resembles employment to capital growth, then the formulae repeat the capital-widening instance. That is, a 1 percent proceeds and capital movement occasions a 2 percent increase, say, in employment. Some capital-widening thus accompanies labor-shallowing per dollar of proceeds: K_z would be constant but K_n would be reduced.

Cases can be envisaged in which $\alpha > \epsilon$, and vice versa. For the former, employment is 2 percent greater than proceeds, say, and 3 percent greater than capital formation. Hence the proceeds growth will be restrained for any level of investment, but the amount of investment required for a given growth rate is magnified. This economy is likely to be successful in maintaining full employment in view of the large additions to the stock of equipment while the distributive forces favor wage earners, with presumably lower savings propensities than capitalists. But the proceeds advance will be slow. In sum, this case is just too good to be true for employment, though too slow on the growth front as to be typical of the enterprise economy. K_z and K_n will both decline.

Where $\alpha < \epsilon$, so that employment grows faster than proceeds or capital, while proceeds outspace capital formation, the amount of capital necessary for growth is diminished: employment will rise rapidly with proceeds, though the damper on investment will make this economy more vulnerable to unemployment than in the previous cases.

Income Distribution

Again, the income shift is to labor. But as capital formation slows up the rate of return will hold up better.

Income Facts and $E_{gz} < 1$

According to the evidence in Table 6.2 a rise in the wage share has occurred; this can be discerned in 16 of the 30 annual changes between 1929 and 1960. In 1929 the wage share, defined as Employee Compensation, amounted to 46.2 percent of the total; in 1930 it was 48.2, and in 1960 the figure was 53.6 percent.

Thus the empirical prospect of $E_{gz} < 1$ cannot be precluded. What is more likely in view of the *near*-constancy in the wage share, and especially the small year-to-year changes in it, is that E_{gz} approximates unity; either values are only slightly below or when they are above, they are only slightly above. While it is intriguing to explore the strong cases of very high and very low values for this elasticity, the practically important cases are those that hover around values of $E_{gz} = 1$.

Automation and High E_{kz} Elasticities

Some earlier remarks assessed the conjunction of $E_{gz} > 1$ and $\dot{K} > \dot{N}$ as heralding a Glorious Age if originally at a full employment take-off but foreshadowing a Desperate Age if unemployment is initially rife. A reduced work-week was envisaged under the latter conditions to transform human idleness into an Age of Leisure with involuntary unemployment absorbed by machines performing more of the work of man. Variants of this case contain some of the attributes of technological unemployment in the Age of Automation.

$E_{gz} > 1 > E_{kz}$

We can review the two vital elasticities, $E_{gz} > 1 > E_{kz}$. To fix ideas, sample values of 3 and 3/8 can be assumed, implying that a 3 percent increase in proceeds leads to a 1 percent increase in employment, and to an 8 percent increase in capital stock.

Income-wise, there is an inevitable income shift to capital though the *rate* of return may fall: this depends on the size of fixed payments as against the profit residual in the nonwage share. Granting that output will increase—and it appears that we must assume this—along new production functions and new cost curves in the individual firms, then what we have is a case of *technological unemployment*. For argument's

TABLE 6.2
EMPLOYEE COMPENSATION TO GROSS BUSINESS PROCEEDS,
1929-1960

	Ratio	Annual Change		Ratio	Annual Change
1929	46.2	—	1944	48.9	−0.7
1930	48.2	+2.0	1945	48.4	−0.5
1931	47.7	−1.5	1946	60.2	+1.8
1932	48.3	+0.6	1947	50.8	+0.6
1933	47.6	−0.7	1948	50.4	+0.4
1934	47.4	−0.2	1949	50.2	−0.2
1935	46.3	−1.1	1950	50.0	−0.2
1936	46.4	+0.1	1951	50.2	+0.2
1937	48.1	+1.7	1952	51.1	+1.3
1938	47.4	−0.7	1953	52.7	+1.2
1939	47.7	+0.3	1954	52.7	0.0
1940	47.0	−0.7	1955	51.9	−0.8
1941	46.9	−0.1	1956	53.5	+1.6
1942	48.0	+1.1	1957	53.6	+0.1
1943	49.6	+1.6	1958	53.2	−0.4
			1959	53.2	0.0
			1960	53.6	+0.4

Source: See Table 6.1.

sake, suppose that output increases by 3 percent, or in the same ratio as proceeds. The faster pace of equipment installation must be interpreted as symptomatic of the technological revolution whereby men are replaced by machines in the production upswing even though employment may rise slightly. The illustration can be identified with progress in the Age of Automation.

Added insight may be gained from the capital-employment elasticity,

$$E_{kn} = E_{gz}/E_{kz}. \tag{6.14}$$

In our illustration this would equal 8/3, signifying an 8 percent increase in capital accompanied by a 3 percent increase in employment. Ratios of $E_{kn} > 1$ would be expected during periods of technological displacement of labor; capitalistic evolution, at least before capital-saving innovations appeared, generally witnessed capital per head advancing faster than employment. Capital-deepening is also suggested through the rise in K_z.

A Regressive Proceeds Path

The Age of Automation can be dramatized more forcefully by considering a *regressive* proceeds path in which *both* proceeds and employment fall off, while the volume of capital increases. That is, though both numerator and denominator of E_{gz} are negative, so that this elasticity remains positive, $E_{kz} < 0$ for the latter denominator, consisting of the relative increase in capital, is positive. An interesting case has $E_{gz} < 1$, with the employment fall exceeding the proceeds fall although $0 > E_{kz} > -1$. Suppose $E_{kn} \approx -1$. Then the percentage decrease in employment is counter-balanced by (approximately) the same percentage increase in capital.*

Fig. 6.4

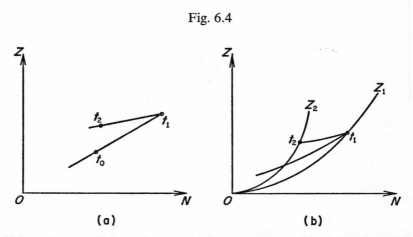

(a)   (b)

---

* Values above and below minus 1 are, of course, also possible though the relative displacement of labor and enlargement of capital is unlikely to deviate very much from unity.

The relationship is illustrated in Figure 6.4. In Figure 6.4a the growth path alone is sketched, with the regressive segment confined between dates t_1 and t_2 which depicts a fall-off in proceeds and employment. In Figure 6.4b the respective aggregate supply curves are attached: the Z_2 curve, which reflects capital-deepening, is pulled *away* from the horizontal axis as compared to Z_1.

Some Implications of the Age of Automation

Clearly, the regressive-proceeds case signifies an income shift away from labor. In t_1 the volume of capital formation can be high, so that employment may be fairly well maintained; still, starting at an unemployment position the investment outlay for labor-saving equipment may not provide full employment. For subsequent periods, at t_2, growing unemployment is foreshadowed, perhaps approaching crisis proportions.

Essentially this is the menace of automation, to wit, that growing equipment will mean unemployment in an enterprise economy which is unprepared to fit labor into new activities, or to act quickly to cut the work-week. The complication is compounded by the fact that the income redistribution accompanying the labor displacement favors capitalists and is adverse to wage earners, and so fails to generate the market demand for the increased volume of goods that the economy is capable of turning out. Ultimately, unless measures are taken to reap the benefits that the Age of Automation can confer, of providing more goods and more leisure as the fruits of the machine age, an enterprise economy will be doomed to wallow in Despair and Gloom rather than amassing the boons in Leisure and Affluence.

Thus the actual outcome, in the circumstances sketched, depends very much on public policy to accompany Automation: the Age can emerge as one of Affluence and Opportunity or it can become mired in Social Conflict and Frustration, depending on the course of public policies adopted and the degree of acrimony accompanying the legislative debates under the lash of labor-saving innovations.

Conclusion

For the growth paths along which $\dot{Z} = \alpha \dot{N}$, with $\alpha > 1 \to \infty$, signifying proceeds advances well in excess of employment, the outlook for employment would indeed be gloomy. The steeply rising G_{ze} would foreshadow a Dismal Age; with $\dot{N} = \epsilon \dot{K}$, investment programs would be small. Low investment totals would hamper the employment outcome while income forces were adverse to consumption through shifts to nonwage earners. Consumption demand would thus be restrained over time while investment demand was also limited for any given proceeds expectations. A somewhat more hopeful employment picture would stem from $\dot{K} > \dot{N}$ or $\epsilon < 1$. Higher investment magnitudes would sustain the present employment level but would not contribute to its expansion because of the implicit "deepening" process.

All along the path $G_{ze} \to \infty$, the income division militates against consumption outlay because of the income shift from wage earners. Only with $\epsilon < 1$, or $\dot{K} > \dot{N}$, can the augmented investment outlay, in volume, be expected to bolster D_i over time. From an employment standpoint, a high E_{gz} or a rising nonlinear growth path will impel government compensatory spending in order to absorb a growing labor force.

Along the concave down-paths in which $G_{ze} \to 0$, proceeds scarcely grow while employment leaps ahead. There is a total unreality about this; full employment can be maintained with scarcely any step-up in aggregate demand. It is unnecessary to dissect this case in any great detail.

The more difficult case is the Regressive Path, in which Z and N fall while the capital stock grows. This is an automation model run riot, and it can only be remedied through obstructing the introduction of equipment or, more rationally, by accepting the leisure and affluence which technology renders possible. Full employment may otherwise be impossible without ample government projects whenever machines, and not work-people, are wanted in the enterprise sector of the economy.

Chapter VII

Income Distribution and Aggregate Demand

The magnitude of aggregate demand becomes the vital matter in validating the supply projections of entrepreneurs in the growing economy. It is thus in order for us to assess the demand determinants and pinpoint the conditions under which equilibrium growth can persist in the march into time.

Aspects of the theory of income distribution will also be explored, for aggregate demand is a major determinant of the income division and is, in turn, determined by it; while we shall ultimately conclude that the income level and division are mutually determined, it will still follow that employment and the money wage—and thus aggregate supply phenomena—substantially determine consumption outlay. But it is the other way around for profits; the profit share is largely a resultant of relative investment demand. Money wages, however, largely determine *money* profits. Modern theory is thus at odds with neoclassical thinking in sharpening these ideas and shys away from marginal productivity doctrines and banalities on "normal" incomes. Stationary norms are irrelevant to the moving economy.*

Wage Earner Outlays

Perhaps as much as 90 percent of the total consumption outlay, even in Western economies, emanates from wage earners.† Earlier we examined the general theory of aggregate demand; here we want to work out some ramifications which are interesting for the theory of growth.‡

First, we elaborate the consequences of the strong assumption that

* On profit levels, cf. Joan Robinson, "The Basic Theory of Normal Price," *Quarterly Journal of Economics* (Feb. 1962), p. 12.
† For estimates, see *Wage Theory and Policy,* Chapter 1.
‡ Cf. Chapters II, IV above.

wage earners spend their full income on consumption while nonwage earners—capitalists—save their full income. This is factual enough to be interesting and informative as a major approximation; undoubtedly it is more applicable in less developed economies in which living standards are lower. As they have done most to promulgate this idea in the modern literature, we can term it the Kalecki-Robinson-Kaldor thesis—though each would agree that it is more rigid than the full facts warrant.*

Fig. 7.1

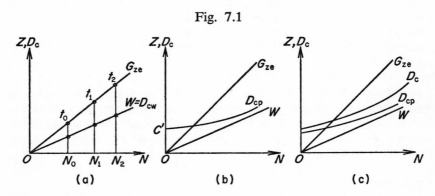

(a)   (b)   (c)

Wage Earners Spend All Wage Income

The G_{ze} curve in Figure 7.1a is comprised of equilibrium readings from each period's D and Z intersection, assuming too that at each interval the equilibrium outcome was accurately foreseen. The linear W-curve denotes the wage bill compounded out of the constant average money wage multiplied by the number employed. As W and G_{ze} are linear, the wage share remains unchanged at each N-level.

Initially, we assume that consumption outlay comes *only* from wage earners, and that they expend their full income. Consumption outlay at each t-date—lettered D_{cw} to denote the wage earner origin—equals the wage bill at each N- volume. Thus:

$$D_{cw} = W \text{ (where } W = wN) \tag{7.1}$$

This is both the "short-run" consumption-outlay function attached to each Z and the "long-run" consumption correspondent of G_{ze}.

Government Employees, Transfer and Dissavings

We retain the fiction that rentiers and profit recipients spend nothing on consumption; but we drop the assumption that consumption outlay

---

* Cf. M. Kalecki, *Theory of Economic Dynamics* (Allen and Unwin, 1954), p. 49; Joan Robinson, *The Accumulation of Capital* (Irwin, Inc., 1956), p. 75; N. Kaldor, "Alternative Theories of Distribution," *Review of Economic Studies* Vol. XXIII, No. 2, p. 96.

comes only from wage earners already in employment. For the unemployed must also consume, whether out of unemployment relief or through dissavings.

Thus, when employment is low, as at N_1, and if N_2 individuals are seeking employment at t_1, the unemployed, numbering $(N_2 - N_1)$ will have to make consumption outlay: initially we can assume that when unemployed they spend about 1/3 of their outlay when employed. Further, pensioners also expend out of Social Security payments or by dissavings out of past accumulations; they too must be incorporated into the consumption-outlay function along with government civil servants who must also spend their income on the output of the enterprise sector. These outlays are supplemented by wage incomes of individuals in non-business activities, such as universities, charitable institutions, religious orders, and various quasi-government agencies. There are also small bondholders (and larger ones) receiving interest on their holdings of the national debt, regarding this as income available for consumption. Outlays of all of these groups must be grafted into the D_c-function. This was discussed in Chapter 2.

The consumption-outlay function will thus resemble D_{cp} in Figure 7.1b; this might be termed the "primary" consumption-demand function for it includes *most* of consumer outlay. The function emanates from the vertical axis at an intercept determined by the outlay that would be keyed for expenditure even before the business mechanism starts rolling to produce vendible items: the eagerness of those with unemployment relief checks, those on government payrolls, and those dissaving antedate the labor hire and output decisions in the business sector. This "suspended mass of purchasing power" serves to check any cumulative downward process and does much to negate Say's Law of "Supply Creating Its Own Demand." In (1) the mixed economy where incomes are received from government and non-business sources as well as from enterprise activities; (2) the continuing economy where there is a carryover of spending power from the past, and (3) the credit economy where purchases can be made without immediate participation in the production process, Say's Law is either invalid or so limited as to constitute only a partial truth—despite its reiteration even at this date in mechanistic models of the economy.*

Saving Out of Wage Incomes

Indubitably some saving out of the wage bill will occur as employment advances; furthermore, the transfer component of consumption

---

* Cf. my remarks, *Wage Theory and Policy*, Chapter 1, where it is argued that the idea of an inherent cumulative downward process is erroneous and should be discarded.

outlay will fall as unemployment contracts. On the basis of these two facts, then D_{cp} will tend to approach W or sit above it by a fairly constant magnitude out to the right. This is shown in the figure. Still, even in the *Affluent American Society* the total of such savings is relatively small in the aggregate so that the wage bill will be closely correlated to D_c-outlay.

Consumption Outlay by Nonwage Recipients

Consumption outlays by rentiers and profit recipients must also be included: we can assume that rentier outlays largely remain constant though they may edge up as employment and prices go higher. In a growth context, as debts and rentier incomes are enlarged, this is another force that lifts D_c at the successive time dates. As profits also rise as we move out in time, the D_c outlays of profit recipients will also expand at successive t-dates. Money wage increases, and concomitant price rises, will ensure that this happens; but for the moment this aspect is ignored.

The D_{gc}-Function

A D_c function as in Figure 7.1c can be constructed for each time interval: each curve reports consumption outlay linked to the employment volume at a particular date.

Through time, changes take place in government payrolls and salary scales, in the magnitude of unemployment relief payments, in the size of rentier income as new fixed claims are created and in the aggregate affluence generally of wage earners and capitalists. The phenomena should work to elevate the D_c curve in later periods.

Fig. 7.2

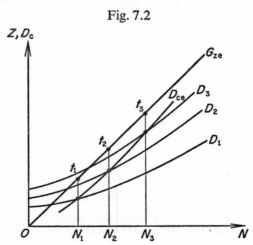

In Figure 7.2 three D_c curves are drawn, with each tied to a separate date. A "long-run" consumption-outlay curve, containing equilibrium points analogous to the equilibrium aggregate supply points comprising G_{ze}, can be traced: thus D_{ce} is the equilibrium locus of consumer-outlays to accompany G_{ze}. Curve D_{ce} should rise to the right and advance at the same pace as G_{ze} so long as the relative importance of consumption in aggregate output remains constant: this would imply a constant average savings ratio over time.

Investment and Profits

We have reached this stage: wage earner demand is dependent substantially on the wage-bill. Money wage constant, wage earner outlay is thus contingent on the employment level.* We now consider how the investment component of aggregate demand affects the profit aggregate and the income division.

Investments and Profits

On the strong assumption that all profits are saved and that all wages are spent on consumption outlets it follows that as $S = I$ (savings equal investment), and as $R = S$, then $R = I$; obviously, R denotes the profit magnitude in a simple distributive model consisting only of wage and profit income.

The implications of this are worth pondering: in the elementary model outlined the investment volume governs simultaneously the volume of savings and of profits. Specifically, the more factories that entrepreneurs build, the greater their profits will be. As a class, though of course not individually, they have the power to control their own incomes. Invest more to earn more—this seems to be the mandate: a drag on investment spending will mean that losses will be reported; this is the corollary.

There seems to be an air of paradox about all of this: older economists might protest the conclusion that the more you draw out of the barrel the fuller it becomes. But this would be a superficial view; a more nearly correct conception is that the more that is put into the barrel—through the investment outlay which creates income—the more there will be available for withdrawal, in the form of profits † and an enlarged wage bill.

---

* This is to state the fact that money outlay depends on money income. No element of "money illusion" is involved for there is no suggestion of confusion between money and real income.
† Cf. the "widow's cruse" illustration in Keynes, *Treatise on Money* (Harcourt, Brace and Co., 1930), Vol. 1, p. 139.

Profits in the Consumption Sector

Sticking to the hypothesis of just two income categories, and zero and unity average savings propensities for wage earners and profit recipients respectively, profits in the consumption sector must equal the wage bill in the investment sector. For earnings above wage costs in consumption activities will depend on the volume of wage payments in the investment sector.*

Symbolically, using subscripts to denote sectors, then for consumption proceeds Z_c we have

$$Z_c = W_c + R_c = W_c + W_I \qquad (7.2)$$

Consumption proceeds thus emanate solely from wage incomes earned in both the consumer and investment industries. Implicitly, this argument builds upon the "multiplier" theory: consumption demand is indirectly contingent upon investment demand and, therefore, the investment volume determines profits and employment in consumer goods firms.

When we introduce outlays of government and non-enterprise sector employees, plus transfer and dissaving elements, we have the main elements determining the profit magnitude in the consumer goods sector. This is shown in the following variant of the consumption expenditure equation:

$$P_c Q_c = c_c (wN)_c + c_i (wN)_i + c_r (R_c + R_i) + c_g (wN)_g + cT' \qquad (7.3a)$$

In this $T' =$ transfers and dissavings, while the $c's$ denote the average consumption outlay of the various groupings: c and i sector employees, nonwage income classes, and government employees. Assuming $c_c = c_i = c_g = 1$, so that wage earner savings are nil, and that $c_r = 0$ so that all non-wage incomes are saved, then consumer industry profits are given by:

$$R_c = (wN)_{i + g} + cT' \qquad (7.3)$$

From a profit standpoint, consumer industries should advocate high money wages and employment in the investment and government sector—and a relatively *low* wage in the consumption sector.

The Rate of Profit

From $R = I$, on the same assumptions it is an easy step to deduce the profit share in business output:

$$\frac{R}{Z} = \frac{I}{Z} \qquad (7.4)$$

The profit share thus depends on the level of investment.†

---

* Mrs. Robinson, *Accumulation*, p. 75.
† See Kaldor, *op. cit.* Also, his article, "Economic Growth and the Problem of Inflation," *Economica* (Aug. 1959), pp. 225-226. Including government, $R = I + G$. G includes government output purchases, salary payments, and transfer payments.

Likewise, the rate of return emerges quickly from the following:

$$\frac{I}{K} = \frac{R}{K} \qquad (7.5)$$

In the uncomplicated world envisaged by the model, the rate of return rests squarely on the size of capital formation, as we should expect.

When we modify the savings hypotheses of the respective income groups these results are of course qualified. But their main thrust is *not* destroyed so long as the assumptions remain as reasonable approximations to the facts.

One major point needs to be stressed in all this. In the economy of fact, the magnitudes R and Z in (7.4) run in money terms.* *Thus both are inextricably bound up with the money wage.* A higher wage will lift Z at each N level, and lift R, where $R = I$ and I denotes the money value of the intended real investment. It was argued earlier that insofar as wage increases are reflected in price increases then:

$$\Delta R = R\Delta w/w \qquad (4.4)$$

Changes in profits thus become peculiarly dependent on the relative change in money wages—labor productivity assumed constant.

A Linear G_{ze} and Equal Shares

The assumptions can be relaxed in a limited way and still yield parallel results. If we take G_{ze} to be linear, so that relative shares remain constant, and further that $W = R$ so that wage and nonwage shares are equal—as they approximately are—then: †

$$\frac{R}{Z} (s_r + s_w) = \frac{I}{Z} \qquad (7.6)$$

In (7.6) the s_r and s_w terms refer to the average savings propensities of the respective income groups. If $s_w = 0$, so that this term drops out:

$$s_r \frac{R}{Z} = \frac{I}{Z} \qquad (7.7)$$

Thus an increase in investment leads to a proportionally *larger* profit increase by virtue of s_r. For example, if $s_r = 1/2$, then $R = 2I$. That is, a \$1 enlargement of investment accomplishes a \$2 increase in profit income. Manifestly, this is the Keynesian-multiplier in a new guise: the investment increase leads to a multiple profit increase to support the associated consumption *and* saving.

As to the rate of return,

$$\frac{I}{K} = \frac{R}{K} (s_r + s_w) \qquad (7.8)$$

and approximately,

---

* In all this, R must be interpreted to include all non-wage income, or thus, the sum of rentier payments and gross profits.
† From $s_w W + s_r R = I$, where $W = R$. Dividing by Z, then (7.6) follows.

$$\frac{I}{K} = s_r \frac{R}{K} = s_r r \qquad \textbf{(7.9)}$$

From **(7.9)** *the profit rate must exceed the rate of capital formation.**
This conclusion is qualified only when $s_r = 1$ and $s_w = 0$.† When $\dot{Z} = \dot{K}$, then **(7.9)** is also a growth equation, with $R = I = S$.

The Single Period Investment Function
Even when not wholly applicable, the simple hypotheses yield penetrating insights into the distributive process. Rather than pursue their study we now consider the investment function.

Fig 7.3

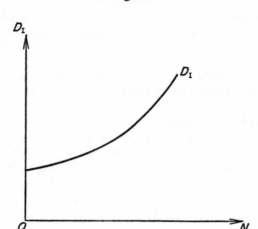

It was observed earlier that the investment component of aggregate demand is likely to rise to the right, as in Figure 7.3.‡ For as employment rises, profits are likely to be greater; this should encourage even larger investment outlay, in inventories and in capital equipment, if each N-magnitude is envisaged in an anticipatory sense and compared by entrepreneurs to past levels of N and Q. Further, when investment is

---

* If $s_w > 0$, this conclusion is strengthened. Likewise, the conclusion follows even when $W > R$. If we associate I/K to the marginal productivity of capital (MPK), as we would be entitled to do under widening, and R/K to the marginal efficiency of capital (MEK), then $MEK > MPK$.
† When $R = I$, all of the growth formulae can be written in terms of the profit share rather than the investment ratio. But this would make growth contingent upon profits, rather than the other way—the correct way—around.
‡ See Chapter II.

projected in real terms, if higher employment compels higher prices, the hypothesis of a rising D_I— function seems even more apt.*

Savings out of Wages

An investment function can thus be written for each period contingent upon profit anticipations and as contained in Keynes' concept of the marginal efficiency of capital. A government outlay function on business sector products can also be described. With D_c, the two nonconsumption outlay functions serve to determine the (N,Z) position as well as the income division.

When we acknowledge the fact that wage earners save, the first consequence of savings out of wages is to lower the D_c curve. Also, profits in the consumption sector are less than the wage bill in the investment sector, reduced in amount $s_w W$. But they are revived by capitalist consumption proclivities, being higher as the consumption ratio goes up with an investment rise. Insofar as wage earners perform some saving, then investment loses its status as the unique determinant of the profit magnitude. Nevertheless, investment and government outlay remain decisive in settling the profit total so long as there are important discrepancies in the average savings propensities of wage and capitalist income groups.

Employment Along the Growth Path

Government outlay in the private sector includes military hardware, office supplies, buildings, highways, supporting equipment, and the host of items needed for the variety of government services. This demand for private output must be included in the D-function.

Business outputs are also sold overseas: export demand must also be added on to the D_c, D_i, and D_g totals. Imports, by and large, are not wholly relevant to our analysis; they repress aggregate demand insofar as they displace home produced items and, by being competitive with domestic items, they restrain price movements and operate to contain the (Z,N) equilibrium.

Figure 7.4 portrays these ideas: an essentially linear Z-function is drawn, accompanied by the wage-bill, W, the aggregate consumption outlay function D_c, and the composite demand function of consumers,

---

* If D_i rises at an increasing rate, the possibility of an explosive nonequilibrium outcome is not to be precluded. See my *Approach to the Theory of Income Distribution*, pp. 39–42.

Fig. 7.4

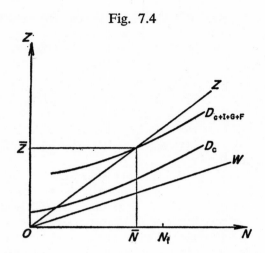

government, investment, and foreign buyers all embodied in $D_o + D_i + D_g + D_f$, where the subscript f signifies foreign buyers.

The proceeds-employment equilibrium appears at $\overline{Z},\overline{N}$. The full employment volume N_f is also noted on the figure. Aggregate demand, in the light of supply phenomena, is in this illustration too small to achieve full employment.

Fig. 7.5

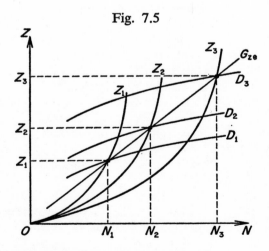

Aggregate Demand and Supply in the Growing Economy

Figure 7.4 denotes the equilibrium determination in a given period; the argument can be designated as "single-period" analysis. In the "multiple-period" sequence of the growing economy there will be dislodgments of both aggregate demand and aggregate supply. Figure 7.5 provides a visual picture.

Assuming more equipment available at each later date, the successive Z-functions will ordinarily move to the right.* Simultaneously, aggregate demand will mount mainly through D_i and D_g. Successive Z and D curves are identified by their time dates in the diagram. Thus (Z_1, D_1), with employment N_1, refers to t_1; (Z_2, D_2), yielding N_2, is associated with t_2, etc. Rather large rates of Z-N growth are portrayed in Figure 7.5 for visual clarity; as increases of 30 to 50 percent are suggested from N_1 to N_2 and from N_2 to N_3, one might interpret the aggregate demand and supply sequence as *decade* phenomena rather than annual changes.

Fig. 7.6

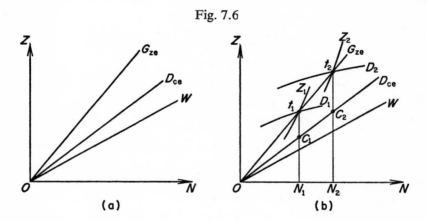

(a)   (b)

Consumption Demand in the Growing Economy

In Figure 7.6a the G_{ze} line remains as the anticipated, and the realized, growth path; W denotes the wage-bill, still on the proviso of constant money wages. The D_{ce} curve consists of the consumption-outlays extracted from the successive equilibrium positions on the separate single-period D_c curves. Thus it mirrors the "long-run" equilibrium path of consumer outlays in a growth context; it is also drawn as linear, implying that consumption outlay is enlarged by constant absolute amounts over time so that the trend of the marginal propensity to consume per period remains steady: perhaps out of every extra billion dollars of proceeds, consumption outlay over time trends up by, say, $900 millions.

Figure 7.6b contains fragments of the single-period (D, Z) curves drawn alongside the G_{ze} and D_{ce} paths. If a concave D_{ce} curve is drawn

---

* This will be especially true if equipment is capital-saving, with less of it used per volume of employment. Cf. above, pp. 31, 47-49.

the long-period marginal propensity to consume tapers off so that consumption outlay ascends at a decreasing tempo. This signifies that more of the business output is devoted to the production of non-consumables such as schools, hospitals, public buildings, etc. Indubitably, a decline in the D_c/Z ratio makes larger non-consumption outlays imperative in order to close the gap. That replacement outlays will rise seems certain: a greater *capital* population will involve, as in population generally, more deaths and the need for more births to supplant the equipment being junked. Government outlays seem destined to increase in the modern welfare economy. So long as capital formation expands, either because of the needs of capital-widening with a greater population, or for capital-deepening to supplant labor in the age of automation, the gap between consumption outlay and growth-proceeds can be filled. This leads us to the matter of full employment in the growing economy.

Full Employment in the Growing Economy

Figure 7.4 disclosed that given the state of aggregate supply the aggregate demand magnitude may be too small for full employment. Policy measures which *lower* the aggregate supply curve, or *raise* aggregate demand relative to the former, would have to be invoked to assure full employment.

The literature on raising aggregate demand for full employment is replete with recommendations of monetary measures, fiscal measures, and various direct and indirect subsidies to private enterprise: little new would appear in recounting policies at this place. Efforts to lower the Z-function involve raising labor productivity or cutting monopoly power; unfortunately, practically every reduction in Z is likely to be *partially* offset through a fall in D. Measures for raising aggregate demand are thus likely to be more effective in realizing full employment goals than efforts designed to modify aggregate supply.

Growth Rate Dependent on Time Intervals Along Growth Path

In Figure 7.6b assume that N_1 at date t_1 represents full employment. Also, that if N_2 is achieved at date t_2 there will be some unemployment. As N_2 seems visually to be about one-third larger than N_1, we can suppose that the time interval is about ten years. Thus while the average annual employment growth is roughly 3 percent, this is too small to accomplish full employment.

Conversely, where full employment is continuously maintained we may surmise that t_2 refers to a date just five years later than t_1, so that the annual proceeds growth rate is approximately double the former rate. Thus the *annual* Z and N growth rate depends on the exact dates at which the respective Z and N totals are attained. If t_1, t_2, t_3 . . . . refer to succesive *years*, the growth rates will be over five times larger than if the same markings refer to five year intervals. While it is illuminating to use *t*-markers to indicate a time process, the growth aspects are obscured until the *t*-clock-dates are specified.

With full employment, a given *N*-position along the G_{ze} path will be reached at an earlier date; massive unemployment will delay the report of a particular employment volume: more calendar days will have to run out before a particular employment target is hit.

Conclusion

As we think through the arguments of this chapter, the income division results from the aggregate demand and supply facts determining the proceeds level. Simultaneously, the income division affects consumption demand and savings volumes, with nonwage earners pictured as having higher savings propensities than wage earners. Thus any factor which shoves the *Z*-function closer to the *W*-function operates as effectively as a rise in aggregate demand to lift employment. Income distribution is thus capable of influencing growth; the contrary is also true, for growth, which is dependent on capital-formation, influences the income division. Perhaps as a broad generalization, in the long-period the income distribution influences growth while in the short-period, capital-formation influences income division.

Chapter VIII

Wages and the Price Level

The wage level, and price level, have been disregarded till now in the thought that price perturbations along the growth path were insignificant. In projecting capital expenditures price phenomena must bulk large in entrepreneurial calculations; there would be little point in implementing an investment program if falling prices promise greater profits through deferring capital outlay until a later date. In the argument that has unfolded, with money wages constant and labor productivity advancing along the growth path, the price level would drop: as the balance of prices to unit wage costs would remain unaffected, profitable operations would not be threatened. Growth could thus persist in the kind of world envisaged.

We now consider the effect of changes in money wages on: (a) the price level, (b) the growth path, and (c) capital formation. Answers to these questions must shape our views on an appropriate wage policy.

Growth and the Price Level

First, we consider the influence of growth on the price trend.

The Wage-Cost Mark-Up Equation

$$P = \frac{kw}{A} \tag{8.1}$$

In equation (**8.1**) P refers to the average of all prices, conceived as an index.* The w-term represents the average of money wages, while A signifies the average productivity per employee. Thus w/A equals the

---

* All elements would have to be treated in index number form in any practical application of the formula. Cf. *A General Theory of the Price Level;* also Chapter II above.

wage-cost per unit of output while k stands for the average mark-up of price over unit costs; it is also the reciprocal of the wage share.

As elucidated in the theory of the multiplier, any enlargement of investment will tend to tighten the labor market and exert some influence upon w. However, in an era of big unions it is impossible to state exactly how high money wages will go.* Even with persistent unemployment it is quite possible for the average money wage to advance so that its changes are at least partly exogenous. Thus while dw/dI is *likely* to be positive, its size remains vague.

The k-variable is unlikely to change significantly, though it may rise with mechanization. Still, the facts disclose that relative shares generally move minutely so that a detailed analysis is superfluous.

The chief impact of growth is upon A, unless investment is of the widening variety in which event A will be invariant. But the widening case is *not* typical of development; it would signify constant per capita output, a hypothesis quite contrary to the historical facts. When mechanization takes place and labor is displaced, A is likely to exhibit its main surge. The nature of capital formation, rather than total output growth, may well leave the stronger mark upon the price level.

Interestingly, capital-widening, so frequently identified with output growth, should scarcely exert a price level perturbation. "Deepening" and "shallowing" phenomena affect the price level more decisively.

A Capital Growth Formulation

To turn the *WCM* equation into one involving the stock of capital we substitute the components of $A(= Q/N)$, and multiply through by the stock of capital. Thus:

$$P = kw \; \frac{N}{Q} \frac{K}{K} = kw \, K_q/K_n \qquad (8.2)$$

As in previous encounters, K_q is the capital-output ratio and K_n represents capital per head.†

Manifestly, a lift in K_n tends to lower the price level. Simultaneously, however, it is also likely to enhance k, and reduce the wage share; from past experience, the change in k can ordinarily be disregarded. Insofar as K_q also rises the K_n increase will be neutralized. Empirically, as K_q and k fail to show much movement, *the price trend is likely to balance*

---

* For a historical study of United Kingdom data, without accepting his interpretation on the theory of wage movements, see A. W. Phillips, "The Relation Between Unemployment and the Rate of Change of Money Wage Rates in the United Kingdom, 1861–1957," *Economica* (1958).

† Q must be conceived over time as the value of gross business output in *constant prices*.

the course of money wages against capital per head. These are the critical factors in determining whether an inflationary price drift will develop. Money wages are crucial; over time their effect is tempered by the growth in capital per head.

Wages and Proceeds

It is appropriate now to consider the effect of money wage changes on the growth path, traversing first the more familiar ground of a money wage change under otherwise stationary conditions. The extension of the ideas to growth can thereupon be facilitated.

Fig. 8.1

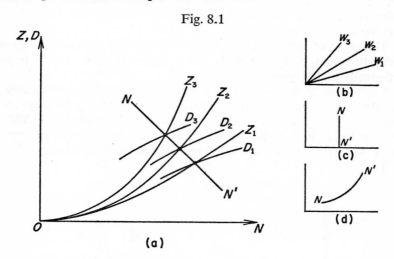

(a)

(b)

(c)

(d)

Wage Movements in the Static Case

In Figure 8.1a a separate Z-function is drawn for each level of money wages, where $w_1 < w_2 < w_3 \ldots$. A dependent aggregate demand function is attached to each Z-function, as $D_1, D_2, D_3 \ldots$, for the higher wage incomes, through the interdependence of demand and cost, mean that aggregate demand must inevitably rise.* The essential point is that every wage rise thus leads to a price rise as entrepreneurs demand more proceeds for each N- and Q-level.

If the result of a money wage rise is to create unemployment, as the classical economists contended, then the locus MN' in Figure 8.1a traces the course of employment and wages: employment will slump as wages ascend. The NN' path yields the demand curve for labor when the

* Chapter II above.

wage and employment relation is transferred to a Z-N coordinate field.*

Conversely, if higher money wages mean *more* employment, then the relevant NN' locus is shown in Figure 8.1d. This is the pattern envisaged by "underconsumptionist" theorists who argue that the cure for an unemployment crisis lies in higher money wages. However valid their argument—and it is a dubious one for an economy interested in containing the price level within reasonable bounds—the ideas are encompassed in the diagram. Ironically, the "underconsumptionists" are really arguing that labor is a "snob" good, with more bought (hired) at higher prices, like mink coats and perfume at Christmas time.

The absence of an employment effect consequent upon a money wage increase is depicted in Figure 8.1c. As Keynes tended to be dubious of the employment effect of a money wage change, the vertical NN' locus has been termed the Keynesian-case.†

The effect of wage movements on the wage bill follows the rotation of the W-curves of Figure 8.1b. Each higher W-path reveals a proportionately higher money wage.

The argument that flexible money wages can maintain full employment through a "real-balance" effect which renders money holdings more valuable as the price level falls, conjectures a locus such as NN' in Figure 8.1a. It is doubtful whether this factor is powerful enough to restore full employment short of catastrophic deflationary sequence.‡

Fig. 8.2

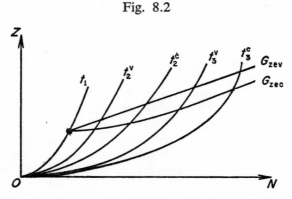

* *An Approach to the Theory of Income Distribution*, p. 112.
† *Ibid.*
‡ The real-balance effect also goes under the name of Pigou-effect. But Pigou, in his final writings, scarcely recommended money wage changes as a policy lever to ensure full employment, believing it to be too weak unless drastic wage changes were to ensue. See A. C. Pigou, *Lapses From Full Employment* (London, 1945), Preface. The real-balance effect constitutes the key idea in Don Patinkin's volume on *Money, Interest, and Prices*. Its practical importance is probably exaggerated in the theoretical literature for usual price level movements.

Wage Changes in a Time Context

Fundamental ideas lend themselves to a growth context. Figure 8.2 contains the aggregate supply function for period t_1; in order not to encumber the figure the D-curve is omitted. The equilibrium intersection occurs at point t_1: the Z and N level can be read off at this point.

On the hypothesis that money wages remain constant, the relevant aggregate supply curves for period t_2 and t_3 are those lettered t_2^o and t_3^o. A family of these functions could be drawn and, with the equilibrium coordinates extracted from the associated demand curves, they would form the growth path G_{zec} considered at length heretofore; the last subscript is intended to convey that money wages are held constant along this path.

Taking cognizance of money wage changes, the relevant series of aggregate supply curves are those lettered t_2^v and t_3^v; a family of these could be drawn together with the concomitant aggregate demand curves. With money wages varying in each period of time, each supply curve is pulled leftward compared to its site under constant money wages. The dynamic wage changes generate the growth path G_{zev} in Figure 8.2. Manifestly, this sits as a ceiling above the G_{zec} path.

Fig. 8.3

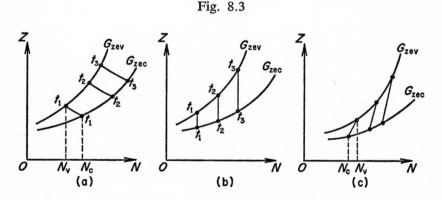

(a)   (b)   (c)

Wages and the Growth Path

Growth paths under different wage assumptions are shown in Figure 8.3. Assume first that a wage rise decreases employment. If wages at t_1 stay at the t_0 height, then the equilibrium employment will be N_c. If the money wage rises, then N_v will be the t_1 employment: clearly, $N_c > N_v$. *The higher money wage thus means higher sales proceeds but lower employment.* Alternatively, a given proceeds total will be reached at an earlier date if money wages rise but, if the classical analysis is valid, it will take a longer time to reach a given employment level. Any prevailing unemployment will thus linger on under these hypotheses.

Figure 8.3b gives the picture for the *Keynesian* hypothesis of small employment effects from varying the money wage: the wage rise will raise the proceeds total but employment is unaffected by it all.

Figure 8.3c covers the *underconsumptionist* image: a wage rise increases proceeds *and* employment. This is a cheering doctrine—if only it were so! It professes universal prosperity with enlarged employment opportunities following upon wage increases.

Fig. 8.4

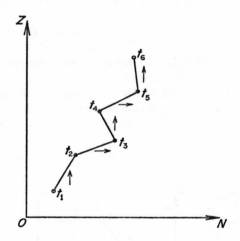

A Mixed Pattern

A mixed pattern of wage rises in alternate periods can be sketched. Consider the ratchet-curve in Figure 8.4. From t_1 to t_2 there is a wage rise; from t_2 to t_3 the wage holds still, and then rises again in t_4, etc. The arrows point the direction taken by the money wage. Obviously, a higher wage always serves to enlarge the proceeds total—so that the nominal growth path is pushed upward—but it can press employment downward, as in the classical analysis. This is shown by the directional reversals in the figure. Other patterns can be conceived, given the variety of wage changes and the ensuing employment responses.

Proceeds-Elasticities and Wage Changes

Once money wage changes are injected into the analysis we must face the fact that the proceeds-elasticity may be fairly large, and well in excess of unity. That is, important relative annual movements in gross business product may occur with employment relatively unresponsive. For example, between 1929 and 1957 there were at least four occasions for $E_{gz} > 5$; for 1932–33 it was 11.4; for 1947–48, it was 5.1 and for 1951–52, it was 5.2. For the 1956–57 interval it was 11.3.*

To make matters worse, once we acknowledge money wage changes the E_{gz} may even be *negative*. As in Figure 8.4, higher proceeds may be associated with a *decrease* in employment over a particular time interval. This occurred at least once since 1929: for 1943–44 the E_{gz} estimate is -2.6, signifying Z up and N down. Although a negative elasticity is not commonplace, we should be able to detect it historically as a compound of the classical doctrine on the effects of wages on employment admixed with the Keynesian view of the impact on the price level.

The Price Level and Expected Growth

The main proposition to come out of all this is that a money wage and price level increase can accomplish large growth rates in money income: this is hardly a surprising conclusion, that inflation can raise the money value of the national output! It entails an $E_{gz} > 1$. Let us consider this.

$E_{gz} > 1$

A high proceeds-elasticity will mean a high income growth but relatively low employment growth. So far as the growth trend is concerned, everything depends upon whether entrepreneurs have correctly foreseen the Z-magnitudes. For if they expect $E_{gz} = 1$, and the outcome is $E_{gz} = 2$, they will have every reason to hasten the expansion. If they predict the outcome correctly, our analysis is as before; it is when they are disappointed, expecting more price level inflation than in fact ensues, that there may be trouble ahead. Expecting prices to go up by 4 percent per annum, while the actual movement is 2 percent, will foster a downward revision of plans.

A wage and price inflation will thus mean an employment lag behind money income growth. But entrepreneurial actions will hinge on whether the high proceeds-elasticity was foreseen. When it is correctly anticipated we are dealing in equilibrium states. The magnitude of capital formation remains a question-mark; we consider this now.

Capital Formulation in a Price Advance

Where prices and wages move up proportionately, and where both are unforeseen, there is no obvious reason for the substitution of capital for

* See *Wage Theory and Policy*, p. 86.

labor. On the other hand, an *expected* price advance should encourage the holding of inventories and thereby stimulate investment and employment: it is always advantageous to produce at today's low costs and profit from tomorrow's higher prices.*

This conclusion is reinforced in many ways. If the price rise follows a predicted trend, then inventory speculation alone can generate new employment—though contrary consequences follow when they are unloaded.† Likewise, there will be an immediate impetus toward present capital construction rather than deferral until the essential day: the "hurry up" signal for capital goods will favor current employment. Likewise, automation to displace costly future labor will be expedited through the favorable current investment climate. Hence, the employment and the growth process will be accelerated. This prospect will be improved if the current rates of interest are regarded as *below* their future course. Under modern central banking practices this phenomenon seems assured when price inflation is predicted, so that there is an added employment factor whenever a price level surge is anticipated. In sum, an *expected* rise in P will compel a rise in N; but the surge in Z will outstrip the N-movement.

Expected Falling Prices

An expected price fall offers little incentive to immediate capital activity; the series of direct and indirect ramifications can plunge the economy quickly into recession. An expected price level fall, no matter how small, is never in itself conducive to higher employment levels.‡

Conceivably, productivity advances may exceed the wage increases and permit prices to slide down gently, so that profits do not tumble. This can lead entrepreneurs to maintain production scales and provide for necessary capital-widening; thus the price fall need not jeopardize all investment activity. But a price fall can scarcely hasten the transfer of investment projects from the future to the present. A declining price trend *must* operate toward investment and employment restraint.

At times, this may be stabilizing on balance, as when population is growing and aggregate demand is rising on its own momentum through capital-widening required by the evolving facts. Otherwise, an expected price drop *must* be frustrating to employment and investment opportunities.

---

* Professor Davidson argues that in the case of depletable natural resources, especially where interest and storage costs are high, production will be deferred until *after* prices advance, and not before.
† Cf. Keynes, *A Treatise On Money*, Vol. II, Ch. 29.
‡ This is not to minimize any favorable influence via the "real-balance" effect. But this is rather unimportant for a small price level decline and inadequate for a large price decline.

Some students of history have pointed out that enormous growth occurred in the late 19th century despite the secular price level decline.* The facts appear incontrovertible. But the period was marked by an immigration bulge, by innovations, and by new industries comprising the mushrooming industrial age. So, capital formation and growth did occur with the rise in aggregate demand and the rightward push of the aggregate supply functions. But it hardly follows as an analytic principle that the falling price level *fostered* growth. Indeed, a faster pace of advance might have accompanied *rising* price levels. The historical record can scarcely refute the proposition that an expected price rise is conducive to capital formation, compared to the retarding influence of a falling price level.

Consumer-Goods Prices

It is useful now to isolate the main elements influencing prices in the consumption-goods sector of the economy and their probable variation under conditions of growth.

The Consumer Price Level

Modern price level theories are often distinguished as "demand-push" or "cost-pull"; both doctrines can be reconciled into a consistent explanation. The formulation also embodies most of the separable elements isolated for attention in discussions of inflation.

Again, the reconciliation starts with the truism that:

Sales of Consumer Goods = Purchase of Consumer Goods.†

Sales are represented by $P_c Q_c$, where the subscripts refer to consumer goods. Purchasers of consumer goods are wage (and salary) earners, nonwage income recipients (R), government employees, transfer income recipients and dissavers. As before, in equational form: ‡

$$P_c Q_c = cwN + c' R + c''T' \qquad (8.3a)$$

In (8.3a) the c-parameters denote the average propensity to consume of the respective income groups. Dividing through by the wage-bill (wN),

---

* Prices fell between 1872 to 1879 from an index of 136 to 90; they rose to 108 by 1882, declined to 82 in 1886, went up to 86 in 1888, and fell to 82 in 1890. Population surged up from 42 to 63 million between 1872 and 1890 while real per capita income (in 1929 prices) rose from $254 in 1872–1876 to $405 in 1889–1893, a move in excess of 3 percent per annum. See *Historical Statistics of the United States, Colonial Times to 1957,* U.S. Department of Commerce, pp. 115, 139.
† Cf. Chapter II above.
‡ See Equation 4.1, Chapter IV for a more detailed exposition.

and multiplying by N_c/N_c, signifying employment in the consumer-goods sector of the economy, we have: *

$$P_c = \frac{w}{A_c} \left(c + c' E + T'' \frac{N}{N_c} \right). \tag{8.3}$$

In (8.3) the term $A_c = Q_c/N_c$, so that A_c stands for the average productivity of labor in the consumer-goods sector. Also, $E = R/wN$, or the ratio of the non-wage income to the wage bill: all wages and salaries, including government employees, are included at this point. The term T'' signifies the aggregate outlay of transfer recipients, dissavers, and the self-employed, relative to the wage bill.

This equation should be of major significance for price level theory. It features prominently: (1) the money wage and labor-productivity; (2) the consumption behavior parameters, c and c', made explicit; (3) the income distribution, denoted by E; (4) the relative structure of production between consumption and investment, shown by the N/N_c ratio.

Many theories have emphasized the disproportionate growth in investment activity as a primary cause of consumer price rises. Equation (8.3) reveals this to be a *partial* theory; in most economies it is rarely possible to enlarge investment quickly and greatly relative to consumption outputs. Thus if (gross) investment increases from 20 to 25 percent of total employment, the N/N_c ratio will jump from 1.25 to 1.33.† While an investment boom of this order can generate a price rise it is not the stuff of which serious inflations are made.

Likewise in most cases E is quite stable: this is not a serious price level factor. The consumer-behavior ratios, c and c', estimated from the study of the consumption function, are ordinarily viewed as quite stable. The T' (and T'') term is undoubtedly more erratic but in the usual course T' probably amounts to about 5 percent of the wage bill.

In sum, all the terms $(c + c'E + T'')$, as well as N/N_c, are amenable to estimation.‡ Each term can generally be viewed as a reasonably stable parameter in the price level equation. (Note that these terms comprise the value of k, in the consumer goods sector.) On this basis,

---

* Included in the wage bill are government employees and salary earners. Separating these elements would complicate the equation unnecessarily at this stage.

† Note that the investment increase will be of the tall order of 25 percent.

‡ For India and its inflation problem see my monograph, *Growth Without Inflation* (National Council for Applied Economic Research, New Delhi, 1965).

See also my *Classical Keynesism*, p. 122. For the investment sector prices, in a system in which the money supply never changed and all savings were used to finance capital formation, the relevant formula would be:

$$P_I = \frac{w}{A_I} (s + s'E) \frac{N}{N_I} \tag{8.3b}$$

But the finance assumptions in this are unrealistic and so the formula is not directly applicable.

the *average money wage* (w) and the consumer goods *labor productivity* (A_c) *dominate* movements in the consumer goods price level. So long as the average of money wages moves within the range of productivity increases, the consumer goods price level should hold steady.

Equation (**8.3**) should make us hesitate before characterizing inflation as "demand-pull" or "cost push." While equation (**8.3a**) commenced with demand factors, in the final theory w/A_c, or unit labor costs, proved decisive. This has only a superficial air of paradox for money wages are simultaneously cost-and-demand factors. Wage-earners are the major consumers; their wages constitute the major part of production costs. A rise in money wages thus acts as both a cost-push *and* a demand-pull factor on the consumer price level. It is a one-sided view to treat either phenomenon as a separate factor.

Price Level Policy

It is probably a mistake to argue that an economy will do as well under a gently falling as under a gently rising price level. The common sense of this view finds its support in practically all situations except circumstances where growth factors are relentless and can withstand the dampening influence of price deflation.

The price level largely reflects fluctuations in the wage level. To control wages is to control the price level. With its power over money supplies, the central bank is able to influence employment and output through pressure on the interest rate. By repressing employment it can check the money wage and thereby exert some indirect influence over the price level—at the price of unemployment. It is a rueful fact that the only major discretionary instrument for inflationary control, namely, the power over the money supply, operates so crudely as to occasion output and employment difficulties for the economy. Unfortunately, the monetary weapons are employed as if they have a *direct* influence. Scant wonder then that in each attempt to impose monetary policy the economy has suffered some relapse; each time the excuse has been that tighter money was required to combat inflation; each time the outcome has been to plunge the economy into the slough of recession.*

This opens the matter of the price level that we should seek, on the assumption that we can govern the wage level so as to accomplish our price level goals.† While our analysis favors a rising price level because of its output and employment outcome, any price level policy

---

* *Op. cit.*
† See my essay, "Toward a National Wage Policy," in *Wage Theory and Policy.* Also, *Growth Without Inflation.*

must be by way of gentle movements, and not major fluctuations in a short time span. All serious price level recommendations involve gradual annual changes. The "scare" of inflation often raised to alarm readers away from a rising price level trend is irrelevant and unworthy of attention no matter how often such mental-inflation of the problem is used by monetary officials in objecting whenever a minor price level upswing is broached as a desirable public end. Their fanciful tales proceed as if an astronomical price rise is intended instead of one on the order of one percent per annum. More than this is likely to be inflationary. On the down-side, a reasonable sentiment would extend to a fall of about one-half percent per annum; larger price declines can be potent destabilizers. A stable price level can be achieved over time through moderate ups and downs so that the decade average stays fairly firm.

Rising Prices and Investment Finance

The profit swell under rising prices not only contributes to optimistic investment expectations but also provides the financial support to underwrite the capital enlargement programs. For as corporations prefer to use internal financing rather than resort to market borrowing, an inflated profit account must facilitate the investment process.*

There is one reservation to this analysis. Insofar as depreciation sums are amassed for financing capital replacements, rising prices erode the value of these sums. Everything depends on the average life of equipment; if equipment is designed to last for five years, the envisaged annual price increase is unlikely to do much harm. For projects of twenty years duration, the rise in prices can be more serious. Nonetheless, the profit upsweep and the premium on hastening capital formation is likely on balance to foster investment activity.

* The relative income shift to entrepreneurs from rentiers, where the latter have rigid real consumption standards, can mean some rise in consumption outlay as entrepreneurial earnings go up. This, too, could enlarge the volume of activity. See Chapter IV above, and *An Approach*, Chap. 2 for an extension of these ideas.

Chapter IX

Technical Progress

A commonplace in growth theory is the distinction between capital formation attributable to exogenous technical progress and that induced by endogenous changes in factor prices. While we may observe the tradition, it can be argued that in a growth context the distinction is rather artificial.*

This attitude can be supported as follows. Higher wage or interest rates tend to induce changes in the relative use of capital and labor; technically, they foster a movement *along* a production function. But they also stimulate a search for new economical modes of production, and thus ultimately accomplish a greater mechanization of the production process: economic factors thus become an instrument of technical progress inasmuch as the movement along the production function also causes the creation of *new* production functions. Endogenous and exogenous changes can thus only be distinguished by a philosophic shadow; technical progress can be regarded as cheapening the price of some forms of capital equipment to economically feasible levels. In this interpretation, the idea of moving along an existing production function is undistinguishable from the creation of a new one. Amassing more capital equipment carries with it an accumulation of knowledge of its use.

Technical Progress and Development

Whatever the causal base it remains the obvious and almost platitudinous fact that per capita productivity increases come essentially through both additions to the stock of capital and through technical progress. Indeed, it is sometimes argued that the two are inseparable

* This is the position taken by Mrs. Robinson and Mr. Kaldor. Cf. J. Robinson, "The Production Function and the Theory of Capital" and "Accumulation and the Production Function," in her *Collected Economic Papers* (Blackwell, 1960), Vol. II. Also, N. Kaldor, "A Model of Economic Growth," *op. cit.* Some discussion of this, and growth theory generally appears in F. H. Hahn and R. C. O. Matthews, "The Theory of Economic Growth: A Survey," *Economic Journal* (Dec. 1964).

and indistinguishable, that every addition to the stock of equipment adds also to our understanding of production processes and so, technical progress accompanies *all* increments to the total capital. But if we do distinguish capital increments from new ideas or new concepts of productive relations, then it is mainly through the latter that the great advances are achieved. We cannot have too many new ideas, too many *good* ideas on production.

The main issues concern the manner in which the new understanding and the new technology are achieved, whether it results from a shift in factor prices which invites the introduction of more equipment, whether it comes from the pressure of higher real wages and the desire to economize in the use of labor, whether it occurs autonomously as scientific education proceeds, or whether it is purchased by industrial establishments at a price through their research staffs seeking to steal a competitive march.

The whole subject of how new understanding comes to be made available to the economic system is an ultimate major matter which may never be answered at all conclusively; the learning process and the crucial elements for technological sweep and progress may have a somewhat different base at different historical dates, sometimes coming as an appendix of military necessity, sometimes from pure learning in the realm of science, at other times emanating in the industrial process. Contributions come from the many sources, from the many directions. All are to be welcome. Whatever the origin, it is the deeper understanding that yields the important productivity achievements of modern times. The full process must be encouraged if we are to continue to benefit from new knowledge. Ultimate imponderables involve questions of whether the pursuit of technological understanding can be done more efficiently and economically, and whether the whole learning process can be expedited. Definitive answers in this nebulous area involving the art of learning are unlikely to be secured.

Innovation and Invention

Innovation will be used as a synonym for technical progress. Schumpeter taught long ago that inventions refer to the technical ideas while innovations imply their use and injection into the economic system.*

Forms of Technical Progress

Technical progress is popularly described as an "advance in industrial know-how." It may thus include the increased labor skill through literacy,

---

* Joseph Schumpeter, *The Theory of Economic Development* (Harvard, 1934), Chapter II.

higher educational standards, or an acquired facility with equipment through experience. Each is capable of raising labor productivity for each employment level.

Capital-Saving and Capital-Using Paths

The case outlined thus involves capital-saving wherein the Z-functions are pushed rightward by virtue of the productivity advance. The G_{ze} path should flatten, implying an income distribution over time favorable to labor.

In short, the improvement in labor "know-how" reduces the demand for capital over time. The investment fall per employee bodes ill for employment although the income shift to labor is a mildly offsetting factor capable of reducing the average saving propensity and thereby favorably influencing employment.

Advances in "know-how" ordinarily provide labor with new forms of equipment, as in a capital-using instance. With more equipment per employee the Z-paths are pushed to the *left* of their position under the "primitive" industrial designs. This will knock income division toward capital claimants and narrow the consumption demand compared to its height under a higher wage share.

The Need for a "Visible Hand"

Conceivably, with a built-in mechanism, a Visible Hand as it were, for assuring full employment at each moment of time, a more definitive comparison of proceeds and capital growth, and changes in income distribution could be rendered. More capital per employee would entail a higher G_{ze} path, and thus, higher proceeds and output, with a larger income share for capital. Investment over time being higher, fewer compensatory stabilizers, whether in the form of lower taxes, lower interest rates, or higher government expenditure, would be required. This is to suppose that the employment level is protected by conscious public policy designed to maintain (nearly) full employment at each date.

One qualification to this vision of an unchanged *underemployment* N-path and a higher Z-Q growth path would follow from the reduction in the work-week. This would raise the Z-sum required for each Q-volume; each N-total will mean less Q. The associated Z path can go either way, higher or lower depending on the exact price rise for each N and the implicit Q. Assuming real consumption standards largely maintained, higher employment levels can be realized at earlier dates and the Q-volume would be better maintained.

Welfare and an Altered Product-Mix

In sum, technical change and innovation will alter the G_{ze} path and shift the date of attainment of N and Z in a rather complex way, affecting the income division according to whether progress assumes a capital-saving or capital-using dimension.

Unquestionably, it is through technical advance that the striking gains in per capita productivity are accomplished, gains out of all proportion to the absolute amount of capital equipment set in place. New knowledge and new technology have won the great production triumphs and the elevation of living standards far beyond the dollar amount of capital construction. It is not possible to have too much technical knowledge: the more numerous the ideas, the sooner they are apt to be incorporated into the productive mechanism and to lift per capita output. Qualifications to this proposition are minimal.

Knowledge is also responsible for the new products contrived to satisfy the diversity of human desires, and to improve the content and complexion of life by preparing new forms of food, clothing, shelter, entertainment, and even education with all its ramifications.

New products make simple comparisons of physical output impossible and permit only vague estimates on the improvement in well-being. When product varieties change, the nature of the economic world changes: a new bundle of goods available to satisfy human wants precludes facile generalizations on the precise degree of welfare enhancement.

These matters constitute some of the most formidable problems in economics. Still, so long as entrepreneurs seek money proceeds and offer employment in the process, with Z as the goal and N as the instrument, our growth paths and the supporting analysis can be sustained. This part is not without meaning however difficult it is to interpret the welfare content of the changed goods-assortment. Welfare superiority must be accepted as an article of faith, for the new goods assortment displaces the old by the market tests. So long as the income division does not change markedly this is perhaps an acceptable criterion of economic improvement. The extent of improvement is beyond our current ability to measure on a meaningful scale.

Technical Progress and the Investment Sector

Some implications of technical progress can be considered in terms of the *labor allocation* among consumption and investment sectors. Suppose we start with a Gross *National* Product split as follows:

	Consumption	Investment	Government	No. of wage earners
Period t_1:	80%	10%	10%	100

Capital-using innovations—assuming that the *Visible Hand maintains full employment*—will lead to the following t_2, t_3, . . . developments on the hypothesis that the labor force grows:

| Period t_2: | 75% | 12% | 13% | 103 |
| Period t_3: | 72% | 14% | 14% | 107 |

The figures are only meant to be illustrative. Capital-using innovations permit an enlargement of consumption output in size governed by the consumption-savings propensities, and the implicit income distribution tends to favor savings through the climb in the capitalist share. Full employment requires the larger government sector. While the consumption sector falls relatively, employment may increase absolutely through labor force growth.

Capital-saving sequences may be illustrated by the following:

| Period t_2: | 77% | 8% | 15% | 103 |
| Period t_3: | 74% | 7% | 19% | 107 |

Again, a reminder that the figures are meant only to be illustrative.

With capital-saving sequences the decline in the capital-goods sector is stronger, with government absorbing the slack: the relative total of resources in the private sector falls. Without the intervention of the Visible Hand this economy can face grave disorders through productive capacity growing at a faster pace than consumption and investment demand.*

More empirical and analytic work can be devoted to these ratios. But they seem to contain the essence of what we mean by capital- and labor-saving innovations. Over time, capital-using sequences may bow to capital-saving phenomena, and then new cycles of technical progress may recur.

Biased Sequence

Biased paths are also possible, capital-saving in capital goods and capital-using in consumption goods, or vice versa.† Thus there can be a relative fall-off in consumption employment with some offset in capital-goods industries. Everything depends on the size of the two forces. On balance, because of the relatively greater importance of the consumer goods sector the capital-using forces should then predominate. Capital-saving in consumer goods should, for the same reasons, reduce the relative importance of the capital-goods sector. It would be interesting to identify these biased cases empirically.

Technical Progress and the Total Product Curve

Since our growth equations run in terms of proceeds, investment

---

* Thus if productive capacity grows by 15 percent and the sum of $(D_c + D_i)$ moves up only 10 percent, an imbalance is inevitable unless government intervenes. After all, this *is* what we mean by underemployment equilibrium.
† See Mrs. Robinson, *The Accumulation of Capital*, pp. 169–170.

ratios, and capital-proceeds ratios, technical progress will not alter the truistic nature of the relations: it will alter, almost certainly, the magnitude of the capital-proceeds ratio, decreasing it in the capital-saving case and increasing it in the capital-using case. In Harrod's equation technical progress permits the same amount of investment to mean more physical output so that a form of capital-saving is introduced.

Fig. 9.1

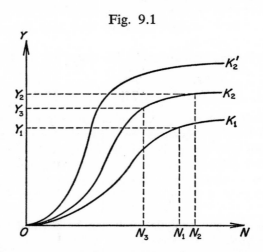

While analyses in terms of proceeds and employment are unaffected conceptually by ideas of technical progress, the same cannot be said for arguments couched in terms of real output. For this is where technological change will leave its final imprint, in physical production rather than money proceeds or employment. To illustrate, Figure 9.1 contains three total product curves. Real output is measured vertically; for the full economy it refers to amounts of goods in constant dollars, arrived at by deflating the national output by appropriate price indexes. Horizontally, amounts of employment are measured. Ordinarily, there is a tendency to draw the total product curves as ultimately descending; for the full economy this would imply universal negative marginal products—we can omit this suggestion. Diminishing returns and falling marginal products are, however, built into the curves.

Curve K_1 signifies a given stock of capital equipment. Assume that employment is N_1 and real output is at Y_1.

Consider an increase in the stock of capital to $K_2 > K_1$, so that capital per head rises at each N-level; this is a capital-using case. With more equipment to work with, there should be a rise in per capita output. But until we graft a theory of employment onto this argument there is no way of telling whether employment will recede to N_3 or advance to N_2: in both cases total output is greater *but employment can be larger or smaller.* Manifestly, implications differ in each case for the Visible Hand in implementing full employment policy.

Where employment grows to N_2 there is some implicit assumption on the growth of aggregate demand in the private sector of the economy. But there is nothing in the diagram to make explicit the entrepreneurial pursuit of proceeds, and the aggregate demand and supply phenomena which promise success or failure for employment growth. The analysis is deficient in this respect.

Technical Progress and the Stock of Capital

The effect of technical progress can be illustrated in this way. After a rise in productivity, for the same capital value embodied in K_2 the curve K_2' shows the new output relations. That is to say, $K_2 - K_1 = K_2' - K_1 = \Delta K \equiv I$.

Thus with technical progress the same increment in capital stock will mean more physical output. At each point on K_2' the capital-output ratio will be lower than for the same N on K_2. Once more, this illustrates the impossibility of specifying capital-output or capital-labor ratios until employment is determined.

Conceivably, the capital embodied in K_2' may be less than that along K_1. But this would suggest that in the economy as a whole the total amount of capital equipment may be reduced while output increases. Conceptually, this is possible; practically, the physical stock of capital *does* increase. Technical progress contributes to this increase by enlarging output disproportionately to the increase in the stock of capital equipment. In this respect technical progress can be interpreted as an illustration of *increasing returns to scale.*

The diagram fails completely when there is an altered product-mix and questions are raised about the *size* of total output under the modified product composition. Accompanying the change in the capital stock the goods contained in Y_2 may thus be quite different from the Y_1 assortment even though the vertical axis professes homogeneity and comparability while none is in fact to be found. This problem is far less vexing in the (Z,N) field where both units *are* measurable and the convention is adopted that more N implies more real output in some sense.*

---

* Real output over time is non-comparable by virtue of the changing composition of output: compare the goods available 100 years ago with those available today. Just how much greater is the present goods-basket? While the present variety is more desirable in the present institutional milieu, just *how much* more desirable is it? The answer to this must be a good deal more tentative. Would the present basket, with motor-cars and TV sets, etc., be more desirable if offered 100 years back, on the roads of that date, without filling stations, mechanics, or without electricity and TV transmitting stations? This is a very different kind of question on which our answers could well differ. On the use of wage units, when once the heterogeneity of labor is recognized, see Keynes' *General Theory,* Chapter 4 for a definitive statement.

Real Wages and Mechanization

Mrs. Robinson has argued that rising real wages and a fall in the capitalist income share constitute a primary factor in the hunt for new techniques toward mechanization and the replacement of labor. Rising real wages are, in her view, the major cause of technological progress and innovation.*

High Versus Rising Real Wages

Of two economies wherein real wages differ because of varying endowments of natural resources and legacies of equipment, that one with higher real wages would be expected to use more equipment in order to economize on the use of labor. With interest rates and depreciation charges being about the same—for these constitute the annual capital charges—higher real wages should lead to a substitution of equipment for labor. This is the inference derived from the usual economic analysis.

Now rising real wages can lead, in either economy at its point in time, to the use of more equipment to displace labor. For insofar as productivity advances with money wages so that prices hold firm, then the money wage of labor will rise relatively to equipment prices and this can foster the substitution of capital for labor.

But consider the implicit supposition here of a rise in labor productivity. In general, this must come from capital formation and technological innovation. *The analysis thus suggests that innovation raises real wages, which then hastens a search for new innovations to supplant labor by further mechanization.*

Entrepreneurs are thus on a merry-go-round, grabbing the brass ring so that they may be permitted to take another ride merely to catch another brass ring which will not profit them even after it is caught. For the new equipment raises profits, raises real wages in the process, makes labor more costly, induces a search for new techniques to cut the wage bill and, in succeeding, compels a new round with the same consequences. In this way the economic carousel runs its circle, innovating to protect profits in order to continue innovating.

Profit Share and The Real Wage

There is another strand of thought here in the suggestion that every rise in the real wage portends a fall in the profit share. But clearly this need not happen so long as prices stay constant while money wages advance in step with productivity; the profit share will then not be

---

* Cf. *The Accumulation of Capital*, passim.

affected.* Where the profit share does decline, it is apparent that there is pressure on entrepreneurs to seek an escape through technological ideas until cost-saving processes are uncovered. The reduction in the profit share rather than the rise in real wages would thus seem to be a force for mechanization: real wages invariably rise with new technology which also buttresses the profit position. But the latter is the motive for making the change in capital lay-out.

Reduced profit shares in particular industries undoubtedly occur. But for the economy as a whole, since the wage share holds firm, the non-wage share, including profits, has also held rather rigid. Of course, there can be relative offsets of profits versus rentier incomes. But for a generalization on capitalist economies we could have more confidence about the principle of a declining profit share occasioning bouts of innovation and mechanization if the facts disclosed important secular shifts in the distributive shares. Present evidence does not support this view.

The Spectrum of Techniques

Whatever the final answer to these difficult matters, the argument that rising real wages affect the degree of mechanization is at least plausible. On the older interpretation there is a shift along an existing production function toward less costly factor combinations as real wages rise. In Mrs. Robinson's view the result is to establish a *new* production function, plucked from what she calls "the spectrum of techniques" to dispense with some labor. Either way the outcome is much the same, with only the quantitative amount of displacement more predictable along a *given* production function. Knowledge *is* elastic. Tested by events, faced by losses, entrepreneurs can be ingenious and inventive. Controversy may be narrowed by the view that movements along a production function embody a "short-period" response, while new techniques consitute a "long-period" adjustment. But if entrepreneurs expect that better innovations can come soon through pressures on the research staff they are unlikely to adopt costly "short-period" responses involving the installation of new equipment earmarked for the scrap heap before too much time elapses.

Expected Rising Money Wages

Putting aside as exaggerated this concern with real wages, for these *do* rise, it is indisputable that expected increases in *money* wages can lead to immediate measures toward mechanization. For with today's money wages and capital goods prices, there will be a given indifference

* Cf. above, pp. 103-104.

boundary between using more labor and using more equipment. With money wages expected to be higher in the future, good reason exists to undertake automation today, to buy equipment at today's prices and to supplant tomorrow's labor which will command a higher money wage. On this view it is the *expectation* of higher money wages that can foster immediate efforts toward mechanization.

Losses and Innovation

Mrs. Robinson's arguments have a deeper significance for understanding the capitalist system.

Those who argue in terms of movements along production functions visualize a collection of known blue-prints, and suggest that cost changes invite a search among the files. For Mrs. Robinson it is the spur of costs, the fear of prospective losses, that engender a search for *new* techniques and the creation of new blue-prints. It is not as if all techniques are already known and neatly stacked up for selection. But to each set of real wage costs there is a new potential of profitable techniques. Technological possibilities belong to the unknown until pressures are applied on entrepreneurs. So long as they seek out solutions, and are optimistic in the process, investment will take place.

Dwindling profits thus become the Mother of Invention. There is no telling what entrepreneurs can do until they are compelled to find a solution by virtue of events. Just as personal capabilities are not fully revealed until the individuals are confronted with the ordeals of life, entrepreneurial resourcefulness must also be presumed to be elastic when faced with some profit duress. Profits can encourage complacency. Success need not always germinate new ideas. Losses can compel inventiveness.

Innovations can thus be regarded as a product of economic forces. On the conventional view, ideas and knowledge live *outside* the economic system and are described as "exogenous" factors. Knowledge is what it is; economic phenomena reflect it but exist apart from it. For Mrs. Robinson this is an incomplete view of the economic process, for information can be extended.

While all this is said, although losses can provide the goad, it is the ultimate expectation of profits that remains the prize. Entrepreneurs must remain optimistic and be venturesome enough to believe that their technological designs hold promise of success.

This is a major perception of the operation of the economy. Innovation and growth become (partly) endogenous forces in the economic system rather than being superimposed from an outside world of ideas and knowledge evolving listlessly and sporadically, appearing independently of economic phenomena.

Chapter X

Optimal Growth

Optimal, as well as non-equilibrium, growth rates deserve some attention; our argument has proceeded as if each growth state was an equilibrium outcome. Also, there is the question of whether steady and stable growth is desirable. Major policy issues are wrapped up in all this and it will not be possible in our brief comment to do more than mark-off a point of view.

Our attention has been focussed on growth in the business sector (Gross Business Product). But the democratic world is also concerned with government services doing more to fulfill communal needs, so that public sector growth may conceivably outstrip private activity. We shall also want to speculate upon the relation of education to progress; while this may be vague, and almost a venture into theology, it does not thereby lose in importance: education may still provide the best route to better living standards. The *Affluent Society* contrasts with under-developed economies in that ambitions in the former are for an improvement in the quality of life under ample material comfort while in the latter, the immediate aspiration is for the provision of minimal living standards.

A Dubious Equilibrium Condition

As an introduction to steady growth we can consider the assumed equilibrium condition of an equality in capital and income growth rates.

Non-Equilibrium Outcomes

Aggregate demand must equal aggregate supply: this was our equilibrium condition to forestall incipient expansory or contractionist forces. Often specified in growth analysis is the condition that capital and output growth rates must be equal.

125

Merely to state the latter relation is to reveal its shortcomings. With capital-widening the extra men require a proportionate increase in capital, while output grows at the same pace. But with capital-deepening, output grows less than the capital stock: the capital increment is designed to *maintain* output, and not augment it. Likewise, the employment advance will be less than the capital enhancement.

Capital and output growth equality would thus preclude capital-deepening or compel an almost herculean rate of output advance, even entailing employment in excess of available manpower. Thus a 3 percent rise in the capital stock which releases 8 percent of the labor force—assuming the new investment is designed merely to maintain the output level—would require a very substantial absolute increase in output and further investment simply to maintain full employment. After all, the very essence of capital-deepening consists of capital growing faster than output and employment.

To illustrate, if we start with $K = Q = N = 100$, and after capital-deepening, $K = 103$, $Q = 100$, and $N = 92$, then to return to $N = 100$, we must have (approximately) $K = 112$ and $Q = 109$. Likewise, under capital-saving the addition to the capital stock may be infinitesimal while output may make big leaps in view of the smaller need for equipment to sustain an output advance.

To conclude, the relation $E_{kz} = 1$, where proceeds are measured in constant dollars, is at best a very special case.

Non-Equilibrium Outcomes

To reiterate, equilibrium in any time interval requires an equality of aggregate demand and aggregate supply involving the intersection of the two functions. For equilibrium growth the anticipated proceeds must be realized; this entails a macroeconomic Z-N intersection involving an appropriate G_z advance compared to the previous period; otherwise, the actual growth rate would either be disappointing or pleasantly rewarding. The equilibrium growth path involves such G_z positions that both period and growth conditions are satisfied. There is thus a dual equilibrium aspect, covering both the particular period and relative movements through time.

Consider the consequences of a failure to meet the dual conditions.

Suppose that entrepreneurs install capital equipment in the expectation of a 3 percent proceeds growth and a 2 percent employment advance. Diagrammatically, t_0 investment portends a shift in Z for t_1, and an entrepreneurial belief that aggregate demand will achieve the intended Z-N magnitudes. Suppose that the actual result is to the left of the expected point: D_1^r and D_1^e denote realized and expected aggregate demand, respectively, in Figure 10.1. (Appropriate curves for t_0 are included, with a huge growth rate shown for visual purposes.)

Fig. 10.1

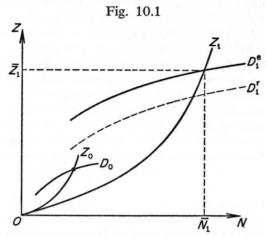

With expectations disappointed we can surmise that entrepreneurs will project slower future rates of capital advance and that the rightward march of aggregate supply will be tempered. Investment is unlikely to respond as exuberantly to erroneous forecasts as it would to results surpassing those estimated.

More, of course, can be said of special factors coloring forecasts; of blithe spirits suppressing disappointments, and the like. Undoubtedly, there is much truth in these accounts. Yet, on balance, we must believe that in economic life the bitten become shy, and error is likely to repress rather than to ignite expansionist spirits. Capital overbuilding is likely to stifle grandiose adventures. Great plans possess a stronger appeal without the memory of a blighted forecast.

The tale can be reversed when events surpass predictions: in the diagram, the top curve now becomes the *realized* level. On the premise that success breeds confidence entrepreneurs are likely to act with faith in their predictive powers.

Conceivably, a forecasting error can reinforce the belief that the original action was correct and that only special factors intervened. But this forges a kind of twisted logic, to wit, that the facts and not the forecast were wrong! In the corporate enterprise a dash of cold water must dampen airy hopes.

Cobweb Relations

The only disequilibrium concession so far is to aggregate demand being other than expected, so that the D and Z curves intersect at an unintended position. But the economy may also fail to reach an equilibrium point.

Actually, this is a more trivial problem. For assume a demand outlay sum below $\overline{Z}_1$ in Figure 10.1. As entrepreneurs have already given employment of N_1, with the smaller outlay there will be fewer goods sold than expected. Entrepreneurs will have to revise plans in the light of the error. This analysis is already part of traditional stability theory, but involving an economy rather than a single market groping its way toward equilibrium. The only new complication is that growth theory incorporates not only the equilibrating perturbations along *given D* and *Z* functions, but also the simultaneous *shifts* in these functions in the course of the process. In principle, it is as if the cobweb analysis of price theory followed *changing* demand and supply functions rather than given loci.*

The Dynamic Equilibrium

Aggregate demand must in equilibrium equal aggregate supply in period t_1: $D_1 = Z_1$. For the output accompanying N_1 employment, aggregate outlay is precisely as expected, to insure that the aggregate functions intersect at the proper point. Employment (and output) in response to *expected* proceeds lies at the bottom of it all, with the proceeds expectation animating the entire process. *Supply decisions generate the consumer outlay sums.*

In the language of growth dynamics we have:

$$D_1 = D_0 + \Delta D \text{ and } Z_1 = Z_0 + \Delta Z \qquad (10.1)$$

The D_0 and Z_0 sums represent the t_0 equilibrium values. Thus t_1 equilibrium growth requires:

$$\frac{\Delta D}{D_0} = \frac{\Delta Z}{Z_0} \qquad (10.2)$$

Substituting G_z for $\Delta Z/Z_0$, and inserting the investment ratio and capital-proceeds ratio for $\Delta D/D_0$ releases the growth equation which is the dynamic form of the equilibrium relationship.

Productive Power and Spending Power

Assessing (**10.2**), it is apparent that growth requires a step-up in both Productive Power *and* in Spending Power. Malthus long ago perceived this union so very clearly.† Aggregate productivity grows over time as population swells and new and efficient equipment is installed. Over time, therefore, there must be a commensurate outlay expansion.

* See e.g., my *Price Theory*, Chapter 19.
† T. R. Malthus, *Principles of Political Economy*, (1836), pp. 361ff.

The subtleties of the theory of growth are bound up with the increment in productive capacity; this is what Harrod's famous equation is about. Demand factors must be wedded to it for consumer (and non-consumer) outlays must be augmented if the output potential is to be realized.*

Measures to increase outlay in a growing economy must thus make a vital play. It is in this setting that we must welcome a well-designed operation by the Visible Hand.

Steady Growth

We consider now the prospects of steady and of optimal growth rates. Further, for underdeveloped economies or for advanced countries under conditions of forced draught, as in wartime, there is some need to outline the elements of a theory of *maximum* growth. Once we are acquainted with the dimensions of maximum growth we can appreciate better a less hasty growth tempo.

Desirability of Steady Growth

Steady proceeds growth is scarcely desirable in itself. Suppose a 3 percent rate is in mind. Likewise, suppose that the labor force grows at this pace. This would imply that per employee *money* income holds constant over time. Faster population change with a constant proceeds enlargement would mean falling money income per person. Actually, proceeds growth has outstripped population and price increases so that real- and money-incomes have risen. Steadiness in the proceeds rate at a pace above the population increase can thus ensure economic betterment—so long as prices remain rather stable. But with a strong surge in population we are likely to view a steady proceeds pace with alarm rather than elation.

The Prospect for Stable Growth

In the enterprise economy the growth rate evolves out of the complex of entrepreneurial actions. Employment results from their response to proceeds expectations. A steady growth rate can thus be realized only through entrepeneurs constantly hiring that volume of labor which secures the proper line of advance. Except through some fortuitous

* Sir Roy Harrod has attempted to complete the argument in his "Second Essay in Dynamic Theory," *Economic Journal* (June 1960). But perhaps his argument runs too much in terms of individual time preference and utility theory. While he does refer to the "Political Economy" of growth, the pure theory of growth omits the entire realm of communal demand possibilities and public policy, confining the theory to an enterprise economy. He correctly points out that for policy the "Political Economy" of growth is the vital study.

circumstances it would be quite remarkable for steady growth to be sustained; capitalism is replete with cyclical phases of prosperity and recession scarcely complying with the image of a constant growth path. Long-run per capita productivity trends which hover within a 3 percent range have not been accomplished on an annual basis.*

Enterprise-proceeds comprise consumer, business investment, and government purchases from the enterprise sector. A uniform 3 percent up-kick would involve proportionate outlay increments from all of these purchase groups. Conceivably, this could be attained in a "widening" economy devoid of technical change and with population added at an undeviating rate. But once the population pace alters, or aggregate supply advances faster than demand, then outlay may fail to complete a constant growth pattern.

Proceeds can then stick on a steady line only if investment or government purchases grab the slack. The extension of communal activities could always enforce steady growth: in principle, the intervention of the *Visible Hand* could always underwrite a constant growth rate. Presumably, were entrepreneurs assured that aggregate demand would grow at a predetermined pace because of the prompt intercession of the *Visible Hand,* steady growth could then become a reality rather than an analytic image. Intricate problems would have to be overcome; accurate prediction, deliberate preparation, and delicate timing of government outlays would be imperative to insure the uniform proceeds evolution.

Barring government action, if consumption outlays fail to advance at an appropriate pace, the void would have to be filled by investment. But this is likely to signify technological unemployment of labor as equipment displaces men. *Steady proceeds growth can thus mean growing unemployment.*

To conclude, a uniform proceeds growth rate is unlikely to usher in an Age of Paradise. It can harbor problems of its own, in unemployment or in a failure to meet the communal needs of a rising population. Whatever its presumed benefits it is unlikely to evolve without prominent maneuvers by the *Visible Hand* in controlling events. Measures of fiscal policy, wage policy, and monetary policy, transcending those currently invoked by the most responsive democracies of the Western World, would probably have to be devised.

Steady Growth and the Business Cycle

Nonsteady growth, it has been hinted, is associated with the phenomena of the business cycle and economic instability generally. Accord-

---

* Cf. John Hicks, *Capital and Growth* (Oxford, 1965).

ing to the views outlined here, the equilibrium growth relations alone have mattered and, it has been argued, these could pursue either uniform or nonlinear courses. When the equilibrium was not realized, further adaptations were imminent. Some of these were alleged to be reminiscent of the "cobwebs" of price theory.

Non-equilibrium outcomes raise issues of stability, that is, of whether a disequilibrium involves a return to the equilibrium path or not. If the departures tend to be reinforcing, what is entailed is a theory of the expansion phase of the business cycle, or the depression collapse, with the "ceiling" being a prominent feature of the former and the "floor" for stopping the downward drift.

In a study devoted to the ingredients of growth we need not embark on the cyclical analysis. The upsweep of the economy, it has been argued, has the two dimensions clearly perceived by Malthus: the growth in productive power through new equipment and new labor, and the growth in aggregate demand. He emphasized then, and the view is valid now, that the *union* of the two forces is imperative for progress.

What the earlier pages have done is to insist that equilibrium growth need not be steady: it need not follow either a linear or nonlinear path. It can disclose all sorts of twists, lunges, fits, and aberrations as it strikes out in a generally upward direction.

This has some deep implications for business cycle theory and particularly for those versions which associate the cycle with deviations from a steady undulating course, whether linear or not. For in insisting that the (linear) trend path of an *ex post* series represents the growth wave, while departures from the steady trend denote cyclical elements, the danger is of an integrated whole being decomposed into separate parts that are not truly independent.* The contribution of growth theory has been to see the capitalistic (and mixed system's) evolution as a whole, rather than comprising subdivided movements of isolated parts and separable entities. Growth theory encompasses business cycle analysis; indeed, *it swallows it,* however eager we are to decompose portions of the evolution and categorize the phases as being recessions or recoveries. In this view, a recession is an egregiously unsatisfactory growth circumstance; a prosperity wave is a gratifying growth outcome. The cycle phases are not independent of the theory of growth; instead, they are instances of unsteadiness in the mechanics of entrepreneurial investment action and the interconnected expenditure decisions of the major economic groups.

The matter of stability or instability of growth need not concern us, therefore, at this point. For these issues are intimately bound up

---

* Cf. Hicks, *op. cit.,* p. 4.

with current analysis and public policy for economic stability. Suffice to say, unstable growth, which leads sharply up-or-down from some reasonably steady path is likely to invite ameliorative public action—or a flirtation with economic disaster by way of inflation or deflation, involving the asymmetrical attributes of each. Stable growth, if we interpret this as adherence to steady paths, entails smaller or larger perturbations which the community may choose to control or ignore, depending on their magnitude and the climate of public opinion. But new and important policy issues are not involved—except for the intellectual remnant which refuses to tolerate the intercession of the Visible Hand in practically any circumstances.

Maximum Growth: The Investment Ceiling

The theory of maximum growth rates involves, in a way, a reversal of the growth problem. Apart from the play of the Visible Hand we have consistently assigned responsibility for the growth outcome squarely in the lap of the entrepreneur: his decisions steered the growth chariot and his actions powered it. Now we turn to a different problem: if we could make growth obligatory upon entrepreneurs, what factors would set the ceiling to the process?

Disregarding technological advance, investment is the key to growth. The issue is then one of lifting investment to its maximum.

An equation can facilitate our understanding; the subscripts constitute abbreviations for minimum and maximum.

$$Z_{max} - D^c_{min} = D^I_{max} \qquad (10.3)$$

From (10.3) the major determinant of the investment volume will be the output level: maximum output provides the greatest opening for high investment. With output at its peak, investment will thereupon depend upon consumption. The importance of full employment, therefore, hardly needs to be stressed: a full employment economy offers the best opportunity for capital growth and future output enlargement.

Consumption restraints will permit maximum investment. A Spartan economy in which individuals were content with subsistence standards could attain a maximum investment potential; this may have been the case in the earlier days and in recent times under dictatorships. Undoubtedly, such systems can be effective for capital formation—provided that output can be maintained at its maximum. If health, labor morale, and productivity are threatened in the process then the gain through maximum investment may be illusory for it could be matched while output *and* consumption were simultaneously enlarged. In an enterprise economy the diminution in living scales that are envisaged for maximum investment can lower the D_I magnitudes over time, for there is little point

in creating capital goods if consumers do not purchase the resulting enlarged output flow. But we neglect this complementary aspect of capital
goods whose purpose is to facilitate consumption output; we assume that
"ultimately" D_c will expand.

Investment Opportunities in a Mixed Economy

In the argument so far, under full employment D_I is alternative to
D_c. But in the *"mixed"* economy government plays its part: it purchases
buildings from the private sector for offices or schools, airplanes, and
military weapons, dams, desks, autos, gasoline, etc. Also, government
hires labor directly. Thus:

$$Z_{max} - (D^c_{min} + D_g) = D^I_{max} \qquad (10.4)$$

Clearly, if D_g can be reduced then D_I can be enlarged. In an era
in which military budgets approximate $50 billions, in which reports of
substantial waste in military procurement are rife, any account of the
investment process as requiring "abstemious consumption behavior" or
of individuals depicted as balancing minute increments in future satisfactions against current enjoyment in response to infinitesimal interest rate
inducements to saving, are somewhat ludicrous; if private capital outlays
are of the order of $40 billions, then a cut in military purchases of $5 to
$10 billions (in an era of true peace) would do more for private capital
augmentation than any reasonable consumption curtailment. Descriptions
of deliberate parsimony in a Robinson Crusoe economy retain the
classical aroma; it scarcely conforms to the facts of the Affluent (Under-
employed and Wasteful) Economy. Investment expansion hardly entails consumption denial in an economy in which unemployment generally
exists.

Optimum Growth

Maximum growth involves maximum *output* and maximum *investment*, with consumption and government resource absorption minimized
in the aggregate. This suggests that the maximum short period growth
rate may differ from the longer period maximum pace. Temporarily,
individuals may be willing to cut consumption, to work longer hours, and
to endure privation, even with an enthusiasm for the task. But when the
only objective is an undisclosed future whose fruits they will not share,
then efficiency and well-being may suffer while the growth rate becomes
a symbol of unrealized progress, with an abysmally low content in terms
of immediate well-being.

Optimal Growth Rates

An optimal growth rate would be that annual output increment which, out of all the possible increments, best satisfies wants over time. In a Robinson Crusoe economy, or in a regime in which an economic dictator makes all investment decisions, or in one in which all individuals are like-minded and have identical wealth-income positions, the definition may be clear enough: marginal rates of time preference are equated to marginal satisfactions from future output increments; any postponement of consumption is amply rewarded at the margin. For the Crusoe decisions to be validated over time, the future must be correctly foreseen: unfortunately, errors can occur in estimating either output flows or future desires; in the dynamic economy mistakes are inevitable because of the inability to foresee the exact scope of technological advance.

Merely to state the condition should suffice to invalidate any simple conception of an optimal growth rate. The planned (or the Crusoe) economy envisages a process wherein all savings decisions are automatically translated into an investment act so that there is never any problem of the underemployment of resources. Likewise, when there is a unitary mind determining the rate of advance, the idea of a consensus or the vague notion of a social welfare function to be maximized are scarcely troublesome matters. But these are very much the issues in the social economy. It does not help to argue that the market rate of interest is itself a "consensus" of the "social" rate of time preference—whatever this means precisely. For where individuals are free to save, but are not required to perform instantaneous real investment decisions, an unregulated market rate of interest may only result in widespread unemployment. Further, the very conception of a market rate of interest involves some implicit theoretical underpinnings, involving money supplies, the volume of economic activity, and the division of income. The structure of interest rates is at least partly a result of the Visible Hand of public policy; it is not, and cannot be, an unregulated market price.

Once we recognize the large and growing influence of government on economic activity, through tax policy, expenditure levels, and expenditure composition, or through laws affecting the behavior of the private sector, it should be clear that the concept of a single optimum rate of growth is arbitrary, and embodies certain preconceptions of government policy.

Vagueness of the Optimal Rate

On this interpetation, a single and acceptable rate of growth which can accomplish all desirable objectives is scarcely definable or attainable; the optimum rate is vague in all its relevant dimensions, capable of meaning different rates for different objectives. For each rate of interest there can be a different growth rate; for each distribution of income, there can be a different optimal growth rate. For each tax policy the growth pace can differ. For every monetary and wage policy, the optimum may change. For each leisure objective the output path will change. Depreciation policy, affected by tax laws, can have similar consequences as equipment is abandoned earlier or later. Each set of patent laws can change the rate of innovation. For each market structure, or degree of monopoly and competition, the rate will differ.

What then is the optimal rate? This is a question which sounds precise in the asking but not in the answer.*

In the private economy, therefore, there will be a rate of capital formation and an emergent rate of growth, given all the factors which

Fig. 10.2

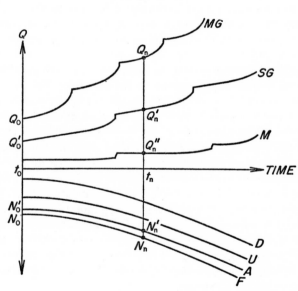

---

* There is one further difficulty that renders the entire concept of the optimal rate of growth dubious in the extreme. This is the fact that the entire idea holds out the hope of future betterment, at some current cost, in the sense of some diversion of resources to investment and away from consumption. This signifies a concern with future well-being, compared to the present, in analyses stressing marginal rates of time preference. But this may well assume the permanence of life, or that individual concern with future beneficiaries is as strong as the regard for personal well-being. It may be that the classical economists especially identified future lives too closely with the immediate valuing subjects. Cf. Jan Tinbergen and H. C. Bos, *Mathematical Models of Economic Growth* (McGraw-Hill, 1962), p. 31 for a similarly skeptical attitude on the concept of an optimum development rate. Similar views appear in Hicks, *op. cit.*, p. 263 and E. S. Phelps, *Fiscal Neutrality Toward Economic Growth* (McGraw-Hill, 1965), p. 106.

influence investment decisions. It is the task of social policy to revise and alter the trend, if this is thought desirable and if it can be done. This invites some discussion of *The Visible Hand*.

A Diagrammatic Version

Before proceeding to the policy aspects, some diagrammatic account of the argument may be instructive.

In Figure 10.2 time is measured horizontally and real business product and employment appear along the vertical axis. On the assumption that the maximum growth rate was being pursued, at t_o and in times past, at date t_n the output level will be Q_n. Likewise, in this economy which grows at the maximum pace there is full employment so that N_n is the accompanying employment level. Thus if full employment is always achieved, the employment path is that lettered F. If maximum growth is simultaneously accomplished, the production path is that lettered MG. This is drawn with several ratchets to indicate the discontinuous effects of technological progress which occurs frequently though sporadically.

A satisfactory growth path in an economy that sets a higher premium on current consumption is traced out by the locus SG. The main difference between MG and SG is that the volume of enterprise output devoted to investment is smaller along SG. SG may be accompanied by full employment or by an acceptable level of employment, involving moderate amounts of unemployment, perhaps in the range of 2 to 3 percent. An acceptable employment path is that lettered A in the figure.

An unsatisfactory employment outcome would see the economy proceeding along the path U, involving unemployment, say, of 5 to 8 percent. An economy mired in a permanent state of recession and high unemployment is depicted by the path D. Likewise, on the output front the path M would indicate minimal growth; this economy would show some slight growth over time merely through replacement of existing equipment by improved new capital goods. The mere "up-dating" of the capital stock enhances efficiency.

The task of economic policy at any date t_o is thus to select an employment path and a growth path; both targets are different though related. If an A path is achieved through full employment policy it is still necessary to select an appropriate growth path, one higher than M and presumably lower than MG. Through time, of course, the choice of a growth path can change even while the employment target remains (largely) unchanged.

It should be clear that important changes in the growth rate are *difficult* to bring about; a rise from 3 to 4 percent is a rise of one-third—not just of one percent. On this basis, major deviations from, say, *SG* may not occur so readily: the various "optimum" paths are thus likely to be closely clustered.

The Visible Hand

For Adam Smith, all actions were controlled as if "by an Invisible Hand." * Yet we know that full employment is not automatically assured —as he thought—either in a pure capitalist economy, or even less so in the mixed economy with private, eleemosynary, and government sectors. There *is* a Visible Hand at work. There is, there has been, there will be, government intervention. The only serious question involves how to use government institutions to influence human lives and well-being.

First and foremost in the operation of the Visible Hand are efforts to maintain *reasonably* full employment, after appraising all the problems associated with further measures to secure it. For example, if further extension of government activity is required to augment employment by another one percent, on some occasions opinions may favor intervention and at other times, they may oppose it. There is no need to try to catalogue the variety of hypothetical contingencies which will serve to favor or frown upon government action.

Once the Visible Hand is charged with full employment policy, and with wage-price level concern, and the balance of payments problem, immediately the appropriateness of the investment and growth rate becomes a vital issue. Some measures to influence investment comprise part of a full employment policy; sometimes they conflict with orderliness in the balance of payments; sometimes they dovetail, and sometimes not, with price-level policy. All of these aspects have to be considered. Out of the welter of multiple objectives and varied policy instruments, the pace of development will be influenced. The Visible Hand, however steady or shaky, plays its part. But to say that we are eager for *maximum* growth is obviously *contrary to facts.* To say that we seek maximum growth consistent with full employment (or other policy objectives) is to say nothing very important. *There are many roads to full employment,* many measures of government policy; some will involve more

---

* The full sentence in which the reference occurs reads as follows:
"By preferring the support of domestic to that of foreign industry, he intends only his own security; and by directing that industry in such a manner as its produce may be of the greatest value, he intends only his own gain, and he is in this, as in many other cases, led by an invisible hand to promote an end which was no part of his intention."

The quotation occurs about mid-way in his book and has received far more prominence than Adam Smith gave it in almost a passing and casual way. *The Wealth of Nations* (Modern Library ed.), p. 423.

capital formation and more future output than other policies. Which route is optimal? A different answer will be acceptable to different policy-makers possessed of diverse social predilections and disparate views on the future against the present.

Per capita growth rates, as distinct from aggregates, introduce population increases. Hidden below the surface are matters of the standard work-week, the school age, work-laws, and the portion of the populace seeking employment. Policies most suitable to stimulate the *aggregate* growth rate may be less propitious for a per capita advance. Extra complications arise, therefore, in identifying any single growth rate as *the* optimum. In short, just as full employment is not a fully unique quantity, the same obscurity surrounds the idea of an optimal rate of growth.

Misery attends widespread unemployment. Likewise, an economy that fails to evidence advancing living scales will suffer in competition with other societies that display more marked progress. Growth thus is a major social target; if reached automatically it requires little direction by the Visible Hand; when it is not achieved, we can be sure that there will be a call for more public action. All that is intended in these remarks which stress the ambiguity of the notion of *the* optimal growth rate is to promote an awareness of the fact that more than one growth rate may satisfy political and social aspirations. Otherwise, the Visible Hand may be persuaded to act, now to speed up the growth rate, now to let it alone to pursue its erratic path.

Herein lies the task of public policy: policy must reflect as well as influence ideas on growth, it must try to understand views on appropriate growth rates and it must seek to translate the vague consensus into a definite public objective. Growth *can* be influenced; the reservations expressed cover solely the idea that there is only one possible rate entitled to the optimal accolade.

Education and Growth

The wisest among us may be those who contend that the most important contribution that we can make to economic growth is not through the direct process of capital formation but through the indirect and immeasurable means of more training and transmission of knowledge. In mind are the intangible improvements in human understanding that go under the name of education.

Education encompasses not only the elimination of illiteracy but also the highest scientific achievements which are productive of new ideas and the assembling of new techniques. Literacy and new knowledge may be as important as extra tools and equipment; some say more so. According to some evidence, the growth in per capita output has been roughly four-fold between 1869–73 to 1944–53 while the stock of capital per head has been estimated as involving a three-fold increase.* Accepting the rough accuracy of the estimates, the computations suggest that forces transcending the accumulation of physical capital are at work. Awe at the accomplishments and glamor of modern technology adds credibility to the probable validity of the admittedly imperfect data: knowledge *does* count, it does promote productivity gains.

On this premise a substantial part of outlay on education should be calculated as a form of investment. Yet in national income accounts the sums are generally swallowed under the heading of government expenditures or as disbursements at private schools and comprising part of the consumption magnitude.† The latter interpretation presumes that "education" is consumed at the moment it is rendered rather than marking a permanent enhancement of skills, or envisaged as an escalator for lifting abilities. Manifestly, this is a narrow view of the learning process however acceptable it is for national income accounting.

Obviously, the insuperable difficulty lies in estimating the extent to which skills are improved through the educational process. Yet there is no denying the permanent gains even if it is left primarily to a handful of persons to earn renown for the spectacular episodes of applied technology. When the investment aspects of education are ignored and the outlays are calculated as embodied in government outlays or consumption expenditures, the productivity improvements ultimately attributable to schooling are instead assumed to occur exogenously, rather than emanating from within an investment process.

Much evidence has been amassed to demonstrate the higher earning prowess of college and professional school graduates compared to those with less schooling. While such estimates are not wholly germane to the problem, they still attest to the economic productivity of learning and the implications for the economy: the more imponderable question would deal with the effect on aggregate real income if *everyone* had more schooling, in time and quality.‡

Education, it must be admitted, *is* also a consumer good contributing to improving the quality of life and human enjoyment (though on some hypotheses this may be disputed!). But this is to inject a more conjectural note into an otherwise earthy discussion.

As others have done, we can face up to this problem—and evade

---

* See Moses Abramovitz, "Resource and Output Trends in the United States Since 1870," *American Economic Review* (May, 1956).

† Cf. Fritz Machlup, *The Production and Distribution of Knowledge in the United States.*

‡ In recent years the investment aspects of education have been emphasized by T. W. Schultz, "Investment in Human Capital," *American Economic Review* (March 1961). The October 1962 issue of the *Journal of Political Economy* is devoted to this theme.

it. For it is still the case that we do not know *how* to educate, for there are various ways of teaching and learning; the effects on growth will thus always be haphazard and somewhat unpredictable and less than fully explicable. As with growth, there is no single optimal education policy. Education will remain an empirical art, imperfectly manipulated by the Visible Hand for improving human skills and understanding.

Nongrowth Investment

Investment in education thus contributes to output growth even though the gain escapes our available measuring rods. Education has its parallel in many other outlays by government which enhance productivity: outlays on dams, irrigation projects, urban transport, city planning, roads and super-highways, information services, police and fire protection, etc. These expenditures, too, are usually omitted in studies in which the focus is on investment in the private sector of the economy. Neglecting the protective and overhead contribution of government constitutes a severe limitation on growth theories which focus solely on entrepreneurial investment motivation.

Simultaneously, a good deal of investment in the private economy will make very little contribution to output growth or productivity enhancement. For example, replacement investment which merely supplants useful existing factories provides a case in point, just as investment which renders some existing facilities obsolete. When this takes place, rather than output growth, there is merely a revised production process. Such capital formation may have an aesthetic appeal so that it is not without some economic value. But this is likely to be substantially below the sums expended on the projects. Only the amount of capital formation related to output *growth* is relevant to growth theory.

Further, misdirected investment means an outcome of less significance than expected: the ultimate loss of the malinvestment is borne by the community which possesses a somewhat less valuable. capital stock than it might have.

So far as new installations render existing capital obsolete, the net effect is to destroy old equipment so that net investment falls below gross.* Where the new products are clearly superior to the old, wants are better satisfied and the product dimensions are altered though the per capita output may not be enlarged. Quality substitutes for quantity. This is one facet of progress.

The ultimate issue is whether the pace of obsolescence is optimal, whether the competitive process leads to maximum results, or whether it does not induce too rapid a change in *familiar* commodity varieties compared to directing capital formation into new areas where welfare

* Cf. Hicks, *op. cit.*, pp. 300-301.

gains may be greater though more risk is attached to the innovations. This is a difficult issue which has never been adequately explored.

All of these matters bear heavily on the theory of Socialism versus Capitalism. Under which system would prevision be better? Which system would force the pace of obsolescence? What techniques are used for regulating the timing of change and variety? Typically, the conclusion has been that capitalism would furnish the best solution because of the direct stake of the entrepreneurs in arriving at correct decisions. But in the nuclear age of rapid technological revolution requiring heavy initial investment sums, the issue arises as to whether private enterprise may not be too small to undertake the vast expenditures that are imperative. The ultimate success of the free economies is contingent upon how well they meet the challenges of the new technological era.

Business Growth Since 1930

While no effort will be made to analyze growth rates in detail, it is interesting to examine the actual growth rates achieved in the enterprise sector of the American economy.* Since 1930, on a compounded basis the growth rate in Business Gross Product to 1957 was about 6.6 percent per annum. Since the Great Depression bottom in 1933 the growth rate was 9 percent. The labor force in the enterprise sector grew since 1930 by 1.6 percent and since 1933, by 2.9 percent. Wage compensation rose by 6.3 percent per annum since 1930, and since 1933, by 9.5 percent.

All the data indicate growth. Whether the rate was optimal, only the omniscient could say. Over most of the period there was too much unemployment. Compared to a more rational universe without war or the threat of war, the large volume of military output scarcely contributed to human betterment. Along with the items of destruction, many of the market products were of doubtful benefit to the quality of life. Frills and gadgets abounded; automobiles were designed for quick obsolescence, women's fashions were created for annual replacement, fads were contrived for fast profits, cosmetics which failed to make the human face and figure more attractive proliferated; cigarettes were adjudged positively injurious to health and well-being. Withal, an undoubted enhancement in material well-being occurred, although less than the gross figures would indicate. The scale of advance was obvious enough to transform ours into the *Affluent Society,* of which Professor Galbraith has written so perceptively. Should the same tempo be encouraged for the future?

* See the study by Edward Denison, *The Sources of Economic Growth in the United States* (Committee for Economic Development, January 1962).

Has the past rate been an optimal rate? Should it be accelerated? Should the Visible Hand move strongly to modify it? These are the major questions for our age. Through it all runs the question of how much more leisure should be provided, how much more of our productive capacity should be devoted to communal needs, to education and to artistic endeavors, to what we are pleased to call the "finer" things in life.

How much more of the prospective per capita productivity should be directed to better schools, roads, medical care, the aesthetic rebuilding of our cities, the easing of poverty, and the extension of modern conveniences to the still underprivileged? These questions must be answered by our society, and directives transferred to the Visible Hand to implement the consensus. Here are the great issues of our day, and there is no pretense that economics holds a simple key and answer. The issues will continue to press on us and in more acute form. How we resolve them will determine our future employment levels, income division, and growth rate, as well as mark our society for comparison to Communist regimes.

Chart 10.1

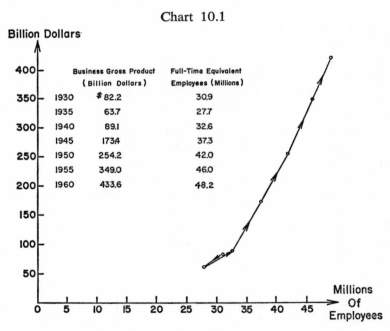

	Business Gross Product (Billion Dollars)	Full-Time Equivalent Employees (Millions)
1930	$ 82.2	30.9
1935	63.7	27.7
1940	89.1	32.6
1945	173.4	37.3
1950	254.2	42.0
1955	349.0	46.0
1960	433.6	48.2

A Note on Growth Since 1930

Chart 10.1 traces the actual course of Business Gross Product and employment data since 1930. To keep detail to a minimum, readings spaced five years apart are alone included. It is an interesting outcome of our methods that the resulting locus looks suspiciously like the curves of growth that we have employed earlier; it takes a compound interest form, rising to the right. Further, the path reflects all of the changes in money wages, tax policy, monopoly, technical development, and all the other facets of dynamic change that affect and afflict our economy, not excluding the structural changes wrought by war and uneasy years of peace. The locus traced is thus a cross-cut of the various static curves connected to form a wriggly upward G_{zev} pattern.

How high and how rapidly will G_{zev} grow? Growth theory is properly concerned with both predicting and influencing this path.

Index